How to . . .

get the most from your
COLES NOTES

Key Point

Basic concepts in point form.

Close Up

*Additional hints, notes, tips
or background information.*

Watch Out!

*Areas where problems
frequently occur.*

Quick Tip

*Concise ideas to help you
learn what you need to know.*

Remember This!

*Essential material for
mastery of the topic.*

Moms and Dads' Guide to . . .

Raising a Reader

Infancy to age 12

ABCs and phonics

Reading aloud

COLES NOTES have been an indispensable aid to students on five continents since 1948.

COLES NOTES now offer titles on a wide range of general interest topics as well as traditional academic subject areas and individual literary works. All COLES NOTES are written by experts in their fields and reviewed for accuracy by independent authorities and the Coles Editorial Board.

COLES NOTES provide clear, concise explanations of their subject areas. Proper use of COLES NOTES will result in a broader understanding of the topic being studied. For academic subjects, Coles Notes are an invaluable aid for study, review and exam preparation. For literary works, COLES NOTES provide interesting interpretations and evaluations which supplement the text but are not intended as a substitute for reading the text itself. Use of the NOTES will serve not only to clarify the material being studied, but should enhance the reader's enjoyment of the topic.

© Copyright 1998 and Published by
COLES PUBLISHING. A division of Prospero Books
Toronto - Canada
Printed in Canada

Cataloguing in Publication Data

Moms and Dads' guide to—raising a reader :
infancy to age 12; ABCs and phonics; language activities

(Coles notes) Includes bibliographical references.
ISBN 0-7740-0594-7

1. Reading – Parent participation. I. Series.

LB1050.2.M65 1998   649'.58   C98-930471-X

Publisher: Nigel Berrisford
Editing: Paul Kropp Communications
Book design: Karen Petherick, Markham, Ontario
Layout: Richard Hunt

Manufactured by Webcom Limited
Cover finish: Webcom's Exclusive DURACOAT

Contents

CHAPTER ONE

Creating fertile ground

We all want our children to be able to read. We know that reading entertains and explains, inspires and comforts. We know that reading provides us with meaning – from how the stove works to how our lives work. We know that unless our children can read, and read on a sophisticated level, unless they are able to analyze and question and respond to what they have read, they will not become doctors or scientists, or know the joy of settling down to read a good book. As we hold our newborn in our arms, or listen as our seven-year-old stumbles over simple words in a book, we wonder: What do we do? What *can* we do?

The good news is that we do not actually *have* to teach our children to read. We do not *have* to purchase a phonics kit, linguistics textbook or set of flashcards. We do not *have* to become familiar with the jargon used by language experts, or borrow a copy of the curriculum from our local schoolboard. In other words, it is not our job to do the job of the primary-grade teachers.

But it is our job to be the school's partner. It is our job to instill in our children a love of reading, to teach them the importance of reading, to give our children the desire to read. It is our job to create the fertile ground so that, once in school, learning to read can take place in a positive way. In nine out of 10 cases, our children will learn to read easily and on schedule if they come from a home where reading is important.

Is reading important in your home?

- Do you love reading?
- Do you read for a variety of reasons?
- Do you have a library card?
- Is your home filled with books, magazines, newspapers, flyers, catalogues and so on?

And, perhaps the most important question you must ask yourself:

- Does your child see you reading?

Children come with a built-in urge to copy the behavior of the people around them. This is bad news for parents who smoke, drink and swear, but good news if you are a reader. When your very young child sees you sitting comfortably with a book on the couch, she will most likely join you with a book of her own. She may interrupt your reading and ask that you read her book, or she may be content to snuggle in beside you and copy what you are doing. She will hold her book in her hands – perhaps upside down – and occasionally turn the pages. Give yourself a pat on the back: you are teaching your child to read.

As parents, we must teach our children that reading is important because it is both fun and necessary. But we cannot simply tell them this. We must allow them to figure this out for themselves. Fortunately, there are dozens of ways each and every day that we can convey the importance of reading.

HOW DO WE SHOW THAT READING IS NECESSARY?

Consider these examples:

- Your son asks to help you make his favorite cookie. You have made this recipe a hundred times and know it off by heart. Pretend that you don't. Get the box of cereal and show your son where the recipe is printed on the side of the box. Read aloud the "Six cups of cereal, five cups of marshmallows" instruction. Allow him to measure out the ingredients. Refer back to the recipe several times to make sure you read it right. Easy? Of course, and you have just taught your son the importance of knowing how to read instructions.

- You take your turn at the four-way stop sign, but the driver to your left does not. When your temper subsides, you explain to your daughter what that eight-sided sign means and why that other driver could have caused an accident. Easy? Of course, and you have just taught your daughter the importance of knowing how to read symbols.

- Your son asks you the meaning of a word. Pretend that you don't know. Suggest that you both look it up in the dictionary. Show him the way a dictionary is organized and then read aloud the word's definition. Use the word in a sentence and ask if this has solved his problem. Easy? Of course, and you have just taught your son the importance of knowing how to read for problem solving.

- Your daughter wants to watch television. Don't sit on the sofa and crank around 85 channels. Open the television guide and show her how to find the appropriate day and time. Read aloud the given selections and ask what show appeals to her. Easy? Of course, and you have just taught your daughter the importance of knowing how to read for information.

Obviously, there are many ways that we can show our children how we know what we know. All it takes on our part is a little thought about sharing our knowledge with our children. Don't tell your son to wear his raincoat; show him the weather forecast in the morning newspaper. Don't complain that Halloween is only two days away and your daughter hasn't picked a costume; show her the calendar and ask her to figure out the problem. Ask yourself:

1. How do I know something?
2. How would I find out something?

Then ask yourself:

3. How do I share my knowledge with my child?

As parents, we are all too often dashing off madly in all directions. It is so easy to say, "Here. I'll do it for you." We must teach ourselves to stop doing this. If the information is available in print, we must learn to let our children find out how to access this information for themselves. This does not mean that our three-year-old daughter can now read the television guide, nor that our four-year-old son can now read the cookbook. It simply means that we are doing our job of preparing the ground. Our children have seen for themselves that reading is important. Our children know that reading unlocks mysteries and is a means to an end.

HOW DO WE TEACH A LOVE OF READING?

As we mentioned before, children want to copy our behavior. So ask yourself:

- Does my child hear me laughing as I read the Saturday morning funnies?

- Does my child see me reading in bed during her nightly trek to the bathroom?

- Does my child see me reading instead of watching television?

- Does my child see me reading as I stir the soup for dinner?

- Does my child see me going to the library or bookstore?

If you can answer yes to these questions, then rest assured that your child will want to be part of this interesting, absorbing, exciting activity that has so engaged you. And so, they will hand you a book and say, "Read me a story."

But perhaps you have been reading aloud to your child since he was very little. You have taught him the joy of cuddling close and opening the magical pages of a book. You have ooohed and aaahed and laughed out loud with him as you looked at the beautiful pictures and marvelled at the wonderful adventures of "Baby's Bath" or "Clever Rover." Your son has learned that reading a book together means quiet time for just the two of you. The soothing sound of your voice and the closeness of your body create a safe and special place that will rarely be found again. *This* is how you teach your child the love of reading. This is how you teach your child that reading is fun, and interesting and special.

It is never too late to start. Don't worry if your son is eight and you can't remember the last time you read to him. Don't panic if your daughter is five and you can't remember the last time she saw you read a book. Start today. Start now. Take your child to the library or bookstore and borrow or buy two books – one for your child and one for you. Go home, get comfortable and open your books. Relax. You are teaching your child to read.

CHAPTER TWO

The importance of reading aloud

Thousands of educators, hundreds of books, dozens of reports will all tell you that reading aloud to your child is important. In fact, studies have found that reading aloud is the most important element for raising children who are successful at reading. Why? There are four reasons.

1. Reading aloud to your child creates a very special time of closeness and sharing. Books become associated with these precious minutes of security.

2. Reading aloud lets your child interact with you, to think about the story and ask questions. "But why is the witch's house made of candy?" A television won't answer, but you can.

3. Reading aloud ensures that your child has a good understanding of books and stories and print before he or she starts school, and will be an eager pupil when the formal teaching of reading begins.

4. Reading aloud together guarantees that sooner or later, your child will want to "do it myself."

Many people believe that if we want our children to be better readers, we must do a better job of promoting reading. In other words, we should think of reading as a "product" to be sold to young minds. And the best way to promote reading, experts claim, is to read aloud. Let your child experience that reading is exciting and interesting and full of fascinating characters and information. Let your child know that reading together guarantees private, valuable time with you. Start early, when your child is most impressionable, and ensure that you have a "consumer" for life.

If our children are not read to in the early years, before they head off to school, then their first experience with books will be forever linked with reading instruction. Yes, teachers will read good books to the class, but our children will be sharing the teacher's attention with all the other boys and girls in the class, the view out of the window, the gerbil, the fish tank, the kid who just wet his pants and the girl who is crying to go home. This is not the scenario that will fire up a kid's enthusiasm about reading. When the class begins the business of breaking apart the language to see how it works – a worthy business, certainly, but not one to catch the imagination of a child – many children will simply click off.

Imagine telling your son that he is really going to love swimming and you'll let him go to the pool as soon as he learns the chemical meaning of H_2O. Imagine telling your daughter that she cannot use the swing until she understands aerodynamic principles.

Now imagine telling your children they won't be allowed to touch a book until they have mastered the alphabet. For these kids, reading will be work, and even if they learn to read well, they won't want to read if they don't have to. But children who have been read to will start school wanting to master the alphabet and the almost half a million words in the English language. Because they love reading, our children will be eager to learn from their very first day of school.

WHEN TO START READING ALOUD

We don't wait until our children can understand the English language before we start using the English language in front of them. From the moment our children are born, we surround them with language. We tell them they're gorgeous and wonderful and perfect. We ask them why they are crying and encourage them to smile and touch and cuddle. We praise them endlessly, and we never stop to ask if our children can understand us.

So why wait to read to them? Maybe you can't hold a two-day-old baby in your arms and juggle her head and a picture book at the same time. But you can read aloud whatever it is that you are reading so that she can hear the sound of your voice. For it is the sound of your voice that is important in these early days.

One mother told the story of being at home with her first child. He was only a few days old and the mother was desperately trying to read through Penelope Leach's *Your Baby and Child,* hoping to figure out what was going on with both her and her son. But the boy was crying and being difficult, and the mother despaired of ever finding out what she should be doing. She finally hit on the idea of putting the baby in the snuggly and reading the chapter aloud. "Now listen to this," she remembers admonishing her son. "It says here that you...." And on and on she went. She was amazed that the baby quieted down and she got through her reading.

But what if you are reading *Raising a Reader* because you have a nine-year-old who doesn't like reading. "Oh no!" you exclaim to yourself. "I never read to my son." Don't worry. One father, who had always left the book "stuff" up to his wife, recalled the time he saw his ten-year-old son, who had never been much interested in reading, struggling with J.R.R. Tolkien's *The Hobbit.* The father remembered reading that particular book himself, back in university. He suggested to his son that they read the book together, a couple of pages each, switching back and forth. He was amazed when his rough-and-tumble hockey-player son snuggled under his arm each night for the reading ritual. There was one drawback however: the son continued to read a few more pages on his own, long after the lights had been officially turned off. The father found himself always having to catch up the next evening.

There must indeed be some special magic in J.R.R. Tolkien, for another parent told this story. "When my son was in grade five, I realized that our relationship was falling apart. He had drifted away from me and I didn't know what to do about it. When he mentioned that some kid had told him that *The Lord of the Rings* was a great book, I suddenly had a crazy idea. I asked him if he would like to read the series with me each night. He was thrilled! It took us an entire year, but reading aloud together every night really cemented our relationship."

All well and good if your child is relatively young. "But what if my child is entering the teenage years?" you ask. How do you start up a together-reading time if it's something you've have never done? Often with teens, it isn't so much a read-together time as it is a dialogue about books and reading. You can start by reading aloud bits of what you are reading. "Oh, listen to this," as you read out something interesting in a newspaper or magazine. Let them comment on what you read, and discuss the ideas they express. You can tell them about the book that you are reading and suggest they read it too. Read aloud a couple of passages that you know will hook them. Find out what they are reading. Ask questions; volunteer information. Is this a book you have read? Tell your child when you read it and what you thought of it.

You can also be really sneaky and offer to read to your teen when she is sick. If she isn't too jaded and world-weary, she might find comfort in this soothing ritual from childhood. In the same vein, you might try asking your teen to read aloud to someone else who is sick – a younger child, an elderly shut-in. Remember, with teens, you are trying to maintain, or create, a bond using books as your bridge.

It is never too late to start reading aloud to your child, although it is easier the earlier you start. Often parents feel awkward suggesting to an older child that they read together when they know that the child can read quite well on his own. But reading well on one's own isn't the point. Most children receive very little one-on-one time with their parents. We are busy, we are rushed, perhaps we have two or three other children. Taking a few minutes each day to read to your child, no matter her age, ensures that the child has a few minutes of your attention, when nothing else matters but the story you are sharing. The book is the magic potion that allows the two of you to be alone together in a special place.

Think for a moment of a wind-up toy. You explain to your daughter how the key-gadget in the back works and she is delighted with the antics of the cymbal-crashing bear. But books don't wind up. You can't put a book down in front of the child and then walk away. Your child needs you to show her how the book works, not once, but over and over again. This is why we must read aloud to our children.

Don't forget: no matter how good a reader your child is, *you* can read stories to him that are beyond his own abilities. You can read stories with challenging plots and characters and with sophisticated vocabulary and grammar. When we read such a story aloud, we give it meaning. The child picks up the meaning as the story unfolds, even if trying to read it herself would be frustrating.

Consider this woman's story. "In grade four, the teacher read John Steinbeck's *The Pearl* aloud to our class, a book that is studied at university level. A poor Mexican couple find a large and beautiful pearl and travel with their baby daughter to get a good price for the pearl. A scorpion bites the child, who dies. The husband and wife return home with nothing. That is what I remember of the plot. But ask me if I can remember how I felt hearing that story read aloud. The horror, the misery, the sadness and tragedy. I cried when that baby died. And you know what? I avoided ever reading that book again. I do not want an adult perspective to ruin the intense emotions I felt for that book."

This woman was lucky. Many schools frown on teachers reading aloud after grade three. Many educators feel that this is just entertainment and that more time should be spent on instruction. When this is the case, our children lose out.

TIPS ON READING ALOUD AT HOME

🦴 Begin as early as possible. Begin today.

🦴 Make reading aloud part of your daily routine.

🦴 Set aside a regular time for reading. Most parents like to end their child's day with a book, but if this isn't possible, find a time that works.

🦴 Select a place that is cosy and quiet and away from other distractions such as the television. It doesn't have to be the same place all the time. Read outside when the weather's good. Read in the swing at the cottage. Read with a flashlight in the tent in the backyard.

🦴 Be relaxed. Don't worry about the occasional stumble or about not knowing what a word means. Let your child see that stumbling is normal. Let your child help with using the dictionary.

🦴 Allow your child to choose the book to be read. Be prepared to read some books over and over again.

🦴 Occasionally choose a harder book for your child. Be prepared to drop it if the child is not interested.

🦴 Take turns reading to each other. Even toddlers will want to point out certain predictable words and "read" the story in their own unique way.

🦴 Let your child touch the book, point to words and pictures, turn the pages.

🦴 Don't be afraid to be dramatic. Growl like the wolf, moan like the ghost. One word of caution here. There is a story told about comedian Robin Williams reading to his children at bedtime. His son finally said, "Dad. Cut the voices."

🦴 Encourage your child to ask questions. Ask some yourself. "What on earth is that little girl going to do now?" (But don't make reading time a comprehension quiz.)

❧ Ask others to read aloud to your child. Grandparents, aunts and uncles, friends reading to your child let the child know that everybody reads. Besides, this is a wonderful way to keep your child busy while you fix dinner for guests.

❧ Try to make sure that it is not always Mom *or* Dad who reads. If you have a two-parent family, then both parents must let the child know that reading is important.

❧ Enjoy yourself. Remember, children want to imitate the adults in their lives. If you're having fun, your child will learn to equate books with pleasure.

- Don't read a book that you can't stand. If you dislike it right from the beginning, tell your child so. (Of course, by the 65th reading of any book, you probably will want to tear your hair out, but that's a different issue.)
- Don't insist on reading a book your child doesn't like.
- Don't tie reading aloud to good behavior. "If you don't tidy your toys, I won't read you a book." This is the *wrong* message.
- Don't give your child a choice between reading aloud and television.
- Don't turn every read-aloud session into a lesson or quiz.
- Don't overwhelm your child with a book too far above his intellectual or emotional capacity.

CHAPTER THREE

Language activities

Although reading aloud is the number one method of encouraging your child to be an enthusiastic reader, there are a number of other things you can do with your child to promote the development of literacy skills.

FORTY-ONE THINGS TO DO AT HOME

1. **Put labels up** around your home. "Miyuki's Room," "Matty's Bed," "stove," "door" and so on. Cut out colorful pieces of sturdy cardboard and tape them to all sorts of objects. Don't worry about teaching the words to your child, simply let your child see that everything has a name.

2. **Decorate your child's room** with posters or pictures from favorite books.

3. **Buy old books** at rummage or lawn sales and use them to cut out the illustrations to make cards, mobiles, other books and so on.

4. **Put up a chalkboard** in your child's play area.

5. Depending upon your child's age, **buy alphabet blocks or alphabet toys**.

6. **Help your child write a book** about his experiences. Did he go to a farm today, the circus, a friend's cottage? Staple paper together and help him tell his own story.

7. **Ask your child to write thank-you notes** and make up her own birthday cards for friends and relatives.

8. **Organize excursions around books**. Go on a nature hike after reading about nesting birds. Go to the zoo after reading about zebras.

9. **Organize a holiday around favorite books**. Go to Prince Edward Island after reading *Anne of Green Gables*, visit Vancouver Island after reading *Waiting for the Whales*. There are many professionally organized tours that visit locations mentioned in the King Arthur legends, or the sites of such famous stories as *Alice in Wonderland* and *Winnie the Pooh*.

10. **Have your children write and send postcards** when on holiday.

11. **Encourage your child to keep a scrapbook** when on holiday or away at camp.

12. **Encourage your child to adopt a pen pal**.

13. **Make pretzel dough letters.** Bake and eat.

14. **Make a favorite recipe together**. Ask your child to read out the instructions.

15. **Allow your child to choose a craft** or woodworking project. Ask your child to read out the instructions.

16. **Ask your child to read a map** or street directory when riding in the car with you.

17. **Send your child to the corner store** with a grocery list and money.

18. **Give your child a journal** or diary. (Resist the temptation to peek in it.)

19. **Buy word games.** Scrabble, Trivial Pursuit, Pictionary are all excellent choices.

20. **Play games that encourage reading** and thinking, such as bingo, Monopoly, Clue.

21. **Buy books of crossword puzzles.**

22. **Play charades.**

23. **Encourage your child to put on plays** and puppet shows. Show that you are enthusiastic about the event. Help with ideas for the stage – the backyard? basement? garage? Will the old curtains work as a stage curtain? Will these movers' boxes do for the puppet stage? Who will attend the show? Can you supply juice and cookies?

24. **Have your child make tape recordings** about daily news to send to friends or relatives far away.

25. Have your child **read favorite stories into a tape-recorder.** She can listen to it at night or on car trips.

26. **Involve your child in family discussions.** Ask for his suggestions when a decision must be made. Encourage him to present his ideas and opinions in an articulate manner.

27. **Encourage your child to play school** with her friends.

28. **Tell riddles** and encourage your child to make up his own.

29. **Recite easy poems** and ask your child to guess at the rhyming words.

30. **Sing songs** that require everybody to add in a verse, *Old MacDonald Had a Farm*, for example.

31. **Become a storyteller.** Tell stories about your family history or about something that happened to you as a child. Begin, "Once upon a time, when I was only five...." Ask your child if he would like to make a book out of your story.

32. **Try stories in the round,** a game where everyone adds in a line of the story as you go around the circle. This is a great game when travelling long distances by car.

33. **Use family photographs to write an autobiography**. Or, encourage your child to interview an older relative and write a biography.

34. **Make lists.** At every gift-giving time of year, encourage your child to write out his or her wish list.

35. **Rent movies based on books.** Discuss the differences between the book and movie.

36. **Suggest your child start a book club.** Everyone must read the same book and then discuss it over juice and cookies at one person's home.

37. **If your child has a pet, insist that your child read up on how to take care of it.**

38. **Encourage your child to start a hobby** that will involve some reading. For example, building a model railroad ensures that your child will want to read the magazines and books produced by avid collectors.

39. **Subscribe to magazines for children.** There are many excellent ones available, and a librarian will be able to direct you to those most suitable for your child.

40. **Start giving books as gifts** for your own children or when they give a gift to another child.

41. **Buy a stamp that says "This book belongs to _____ ."** Let your child stamp all of his or her books.

CHAPTER FOUR

Baby steps:
The infant reader

You have arrived home from the hospital with your newborn. You now have thousands of decisions to make about issues you've never had to think about before. Cloth diapers or disposables? Breast or bottle feeding? Soothers or thumbs? Then there are the issues that you don't have to think about for years, but that every parent lies awake at night worrying about anyway. How will I teach him not to drink and drive? Do I send him to a private school? What if she's a drop-out? What if he gets sick?

Parents know that they can make themselves sick worrying about the next 20 years of a three-day-old's life. So here is one issue that you don't have to worry about or think about.

Parents often feel awkward reading aloud to someone who doesn't seem to understand a word of what they are saying. It is almost as if they've been caught talking out loud to themselves. But this is very far from the truth. Scientists have done numerous studies that show that babies only a few days old can pick out the sound of their mother's voice from amongst many others. Crying newborns will stop and turn their eyes toward the voice they know best.

When you hold your newborn in your arms and read, you are calming and comforting your child with both your voice and your body, enveloping your child in a sense of well-being. Your reading voice takes on a rhythmic sound that is different from your everyday voice, and your child begins to recognize this special voice as well.

Does it matter what you read in these early days? Probably not. Remember the mother in Chapter 2 who told of reading the child-care book to her newborn. The baby calmed down because he was in her arms, listening to her voice. So read tonight's dinner recipe out loud to your child. Read today's newspaper or magazine. Read your own book of escape fiction or scholarly treatise. The important points are these:

- You are surrounding your child with the sound of your voice.
- You are preparing both of you for the reading aloud that lies ahead.

Very soon, however, your child will be a newborn no longer. He will be lifting his head and looking for you. He will be rolling over and struggling to sit up. He will splash about in a bathtub and start getting food from tray to mouth. Now is when the words you read becomes magical.

 Read to your baby. Simple, right? No need to choose, to ponder, to weigh the odds, to debate with in-laws. Read to your baby and know that you are giving your child a gift that will enrich life more than anything else.

Reading aloud at this stage still doesn't have much to do with the actual words on the page. It has to do with playing and the child's recognition of self. This is when you begin reading nursery rhymes and simple baby books that are (surprise, surprise) all about a baby's world. Think of some of the Mother Goose rhymes. *Rub-a-dub-dub* tells your baby about the bathtub. *Humpty Dumpty* and *London Bridge* are both about falling down, something that six-month-olds are becoming very familiar with. *Pat-a-cake* and *Little Jack Horner* are about eating. These are the stories that tell babies about themselves, that let them recognize themselves in stories. And the best part about reading such nursery rhymes is that we, tired, busy parents, can remember them. We don't need the book to call out "Humpty Dumpty had a great fall!" as we let baby slide down our knee and be caught just in the nick of time. Or as you put your child in her high chair, why not sing out, "Little Miss Muffet, sat on a tuffet." And you don't need a book to recite *This Little Pig* as you count off your child's toes.

There are many wonderful baby books to choose from. Most of these are board books – books made with heavy cardboard pages to withstand heavy wear and tear – or plastic books that can be chewed and drooled on and even go into the bathtub. These are the books that can be left in the crib or playpen and won't harm or be damaged. There will probably be only a few words on each page, or maybe no words at all. The pictures will be simple, bright and bold. While your child is attracted to the picture of a big colorful shoe, you can be reciting *One, Two, Buckle My Shoe*. You can be asking those all important questions: "And where is baby's shoe? Is it here? (Tickle nose.) Is it here? (Tickle tummy.) Here it is! (Tickle toes.)"

Reading to your child at this age is all about being together and playing with words and rhymes and pictures. It is about cuddling and tickling and exploring. It is about allowing your child to see her life reflected in the pages of a book. It is also about learning the rhythm of the language. This is one of the reasons why Mother Goose is still around and why publishing companies seem to bring out new versions almost every year. The stories are about a baby's world, and they use rhythmic, rhyming, rollicking language to describe this world. What baby can resist:

> *Jeremiah, blow the fire*
> *Puff, puff, puff!*
> *First you blow it gently,*
> *Then you blow it rough!*

Of course, you should be matching action to word with lots of huffing and puffing in the baby's face. When you do so, or when you count toes, or walk your fingers up the baby's face for *Hickory, Dickory, Dock*, you are giving your child the opportunity to participate in the movement, game, or song. Your child is learning that books are interactive. Remember:

• Infants like nursery rhymes with lots of action.

- Infants will imitate the actions of the rhymes or stories (clapping of hands, wiggling of toes).
- Infants will repeat the sounds in the stories (the moo of the cow, bark of the dog).
- Infants like repetition and rhythm.
- Infants need to see babies in books. They recognize someone like themselves.

Best Books for Babies
What to Look For

- simple language
- lots of repetition of sounds and words
- topics of interest to your child – bedtime, bathtime and so on
- simple, colorful illustrations
- books sized to fit baby's hands
- sturdy books that will stand up to being chewed and dropped

SOME FAVORITE BOOKS FOR BABIES

Goodnight Moon, by Margaret Wise Brown and Clement Hurd, Harper, 1947, 1977. Every child will copy the bunny's bedtime ritual of saying goodnight to everything in the bedroom.

Here's Baabee, by Dayal Kaur Khalsa, Tundra Books, 1983. There are several boardbooks in this series showing Baabee involved in everyday activities.

I Can, by Helen Oxenbury, Walker, 1985. One of several titles by this well-known British artist. A baby discovers a world of new delights.

Lollipop's Room (and other titles), by Micheline Chartrand and Helene Desputeaux, Editions Chouette Inc., 1994. This series of books show balloon-faced baby Lollipop's emotions.

My Very First Mother Goose, by Iona Opie and Rosemary Wells, Candlewick Press, 1996. A gorgeously illustrated, first-class collection of favorite rhymes.

The New Baby Calf, by Edith N. Chase and Barbara Reid, Scholastic, 1984. Buttercup the cow has a new baby that grows strong by the end of the story. Illustrated with Reid's wonderful Plasticine art.

One, Two, Buckle My Shoe, by Heather Collins, Kids Can Press, 1997. In this version of the well-known nursery rhyme, Collins explains why everyone is buckling shoes and picking up sticks. Three other titles in the series: *Eensy Weensy Spider, Hickory Dickory Dock, This Little Piggy*.

Zoe's Sunny Day, by Barbara Reid, Scholastic, 1991. One of four wordless books that takes a baby through the seasons.

CHAPTER FIVE

Terrific twos:
Your toddler "reads"

Somewhere around two years of age, a child's language skills undergo a dramatic development. It is as if your child has been collecting hundreds of words over the first few months of his life and suddenly bursts forth with an incredible vocabulary. This is also the time that our children begin to show mastery over their environment. They can walk from here to there - they don't have to wait for the busy adult to hear their cry and pick them up. They can ask for specific food items and choose their own clothes and toys. They frequently use the "n" word - "No!" - to let us know that they have their own opinion about everything. This is the stage fondly referred to as "the terrible twos" because children can now exert some control over their lives.

As children gain confidence and learn to manipulate the world around them, their imagination thrives and their curiosity grows. A smart parent will direct some of this boundless enthusiasm toward books. If you haven't been reading to your child, it is very important that you start now. Remember, most children at the age of two are beginning to watch television, and it will become more and more difficult for you to convince your child of the joys of reading, if television is the only form of entertainment in your home.

EARLY SIGNS OF READING

What really happens at this stage of learning how to read? One mother told this interesting story. "My husband and I were in the living room, reading books. Our two-year-old wandered in and stood looking at us. I didn't say anything – I was hoping he wouldn't interrupt me because I was at a great point in my book. I watched my son out of the corner of my eye. Soon, he picked up one of his books, and sat down on the couch. He held the book in his hands and carefully turned the pages, moving his head back and forth. I was amused to see that he was watching me out of the corner of his eye, not wanting to let on that he didn't really know how to play this new game. And I suddenly realized that we were teaching our child to read."

This is reading, you ask? Yes. Remember, children learn by imitating and, by imitating you reading, they are beginning to make sense out of a book. Making sense of a book involves the following. Your child:

- holds the book the right way up
- turns the pages
- looks at the words and studies the pictures
- uses the pictures to make up a new version of the story
- selects favorite books by name ("I want to read *Red Is Best*.")
- wants to read favorite books over and over again
- shows a curiosity about words ("What does this say?")
- makes connections between the book and her life ("I like red best, too!")

Some of us still have difficulty accepting all this as learning how to read. We think of reading in terms of word attack skills and phonics. But these are the tools a child needs to decode reading material later on. These tools do not give us a love of reading. When you realize that a number of children enter school without the least idea of how a book works or why reading is interesting, you can imagine the uphill battle the teachers face when they begin reading instruction.

❧ Read to your child every day.

❧ Let your child see you reading every day.

❧ Make sure your child has a library card.

❧ Make going to the library a routine event.

❧ Select books that mirror your child's life.

❧ Let your child pick out the book he wants to read.

❧ Let your child hold the book and turn the pages.

❧ Praise your child's attempts to read the book.

❧ Take books with you wherever you go.

❧ Talk about the stories you have read.

❧ Talk about the illustrations in the book.

❧ Play cassettes of authors reading their own stories.

❧ Combine a book with an activity. For example, visit the zoo after reading a book about baby animals.

❧ Leave books all around your home (bedrooms, living room, kitchen, bathroom, tool room).

Best Books for Toddlers
What to Look For

- topics that deal with familiar situations
- topics that expand your child's knowledge
- stories that enhance your child's vocabulary
- stories, poems and verse that encourage your child to have fun with words
- repetitive bits for joining in
- silly nonsense stories to challenge your child's sense of the "real" world

SOME FAVORITE BOOKS FOR TODDLERS

The Bare Naked Book, by Kathy Stinson and Heather Collins, Annick Press, 1986. A delightful way of showing all parts of all bodies.

Big or Little, by Kathy Stinson and Robin Baird Lewis, Annick Press, 1983. A child is confused about whether he is all grown up or still very young.

By the Sea: An Alphabet Book, by Ann Blades, Kids Can Press, 1985. This ABC book shows two little children at the seaside from morning to night. It is a work of art.

Miffy, by Dick Bruna, Methuen, 1967. This delightful character takes the reader through the many experiences of childhood. Several titles in series.

Numbers of Things, by Helen Oxenbury, Heinemann, 1967. This counting book remains a favorite for its colorful pages depicting numbers from one to 50.

Red Is Best, by Kathy Stinson and Robin Baird Lewis, Annick Press, 1982. A child defends her love of the color red.

Toilet Tales, by Andrea Wayne von Konigslow, Annick Press, 1985. This silly lesson explains to children why toilets are for people and not animals, fish or any other type of critter.

CHAPTER SIX

"I'll do it myself!" Your preschooler "reads."

When your child is four or five years old, she has not only figured out how to hold a book and turn the pages, but has also memorized favorite stories and will try to match spoken words to the written words in the book. She knows that the story is always the same each time that the book is read, and so she will feel comfortable experimenting with reading. Remember: your child's accuracy at this stage doesn't matter. It is her enthusiasm which is so important.

One father told of watching his son doing just this with the book *Brown Bear, Brown Bear*, by Bill Martin Jr. The text begins, "Brown bear, brown bear, what do you see? I see a red bird looking at me." The next page reads, "Red bird, red bird, what do you see? I see a...looking at me." The boy could read each page of the book except the new word on each page, in this first example, red bird. But he knew that the picture on the next page would tell him what the bear sees, what the red bird sees and so on. The father soon noticed that his son was very carefully sneaking a peek at the next page so that he could "read" the story. The boy was experimenting with reading because he knew it was a safe thing to do.

It is very easy for parents who are not experts in early child education to be unaware of the dramatic achievement of this little boy. To them, this isn't really reading: it is memory and guesswork. But consider what the child was demonstrating:

1. He had learned that the book had a pattern.
2. He had learned that he could predict the pattern.

3. He had learned that he could look for clues in the story and pictures to help him understand the words.
4. He had learned that the picture of the red bird matched the letters r-e-d b-i-r-d, and so on throughout the book.

An extra bonus for this family was the fact that there was a sibling. Feeling safe about tackling this book, the boy was excited about reading to his younger sister. This in turn guaranteed that the sister would want to be a reader as well – the "Me too!" attitude in action.

This boy had also learned that books don't change. The story is always the same. This offers children consistency and security, and that is why children love to hear the same story over and over again. At this stage in their lives, they need to know that some things won't change. A favorite story, read dozens of times, is a security blanket.

A woman who doesn't have children related the following story: "I was reading one of my four-year-old niece's favorite books and I got to the word 'trousers.' I thought nobody says trousers nowadays, so I changed the word to 'pants.' Well! My niece told me in no uncertain terms that this word – and she pointed to 'trousers' – says trousers. I'll never forget the look of scorn she gave me. I learned a valuable lesson that day."

Children in this experimental stage of reading are also ready for books that have setting, plot and character development. The setting can be as simple as "Far, far away, and long, long ago." Children who are four or five are beginning to have an understanding of the concepts of time and place. They know that they have to wait 10 more days for their birthday, and that Grandma lives a half-day car ride away. They also understand that some people live in different parts of the world. If you read a book taking place in a faraway land, you can find a map or use a globe to teach your child something about distance and geography. "Remember how long it took us to go to Aunt Ruth's cottage? Well it would take five whole days to drive to the place in this story."

Children now understand plot. They know stories have a beginning, a middle and an ending. They understand that some sort of problem is usually introduced at the beginning of a story and that this problem must be solved before the book ends. They expect some build-up of tension. Consider one favorite troublemaker: the Cat in the Hat. The children in the story are bored, the cat shows up and creates chaos. Will the house be in order before the mother returns home? Will the children get into trouble? Of course not. All is well by the end of the story. This plot appears deceptively simple, but it follows the same format as the most complicated Shakespearean comedy.

Some books for children this age offer quite a bit of character development. In *Franklin in the Dark*, by Paulette Bourgeois, Franklin learns how to overcome his fear of the dark, and becomes a more confident creature. In Maurice Sendak's *Where the Wild Things Are*, Max learns how to tame his own wild temper. Although not all books show a character growing in some way, books for this age level must create real characters, with real names. Your child is no longer content with "Baby has bath. Baby gets dried off. Baby puts on pajamas." Our children are now demanding much more sophistication in their books.

HOW TO HELP YOUR PRESCHOOL CHILD

- Read to your child every day.

- Let your child see you reading every day.

- Make sure your child has a library card.

- Let your child read the story to you.

- Discuss the story as you go.

- Discuss the illustrations.

- Talk about the characters, plot and setting.

- Use "book language" whenever possible. Refer to the cover, the page, the title page, the author's name, the illustrator's name and so on.

- Compare the people or events in a book to similar events in your own life.

- If financially feasible, allow your child to buy a book every now and then.

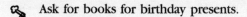
Ask for books for birthday presents.

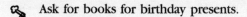
Let your children print their names in books that belong to them.

Best Books for Preschoolers
What to Look For

• Stories that both confirm and expand your child's understanding of the world.

• Stories that have an intriguing plot and interesting characters.

• Stories that suggest the great themes of literature: sorrow, struggle, love, anger and so on.

• Stories that expand your child's vocabulary.

• Themes that appeal to your child.

• Books with detailed and imaginative illustrations.

• Books of poetry and rhyme.

• Books with two to four sentences per page.

• Stories that use rhythm, rhyme or logic to help the child read.

SOME FAVORITE BOOKS FOR PRESCHOOLERS

Amos's Sweater, by Janet Lunn and Kim LaFave, Groundwood, 1988. Amos the sheep is tired of giving away all his wool. The solution is delightful.

Franklin in the Dark, by Paulette Bourgeois and Brenda Clark, Kids Can Press, 1986. Franklin overcomes his fear of sleeping alone in his small, dark shell. The first book in a series that deals with the problems and joys of being young.

Jeremiah and Mrs. Ming, by Sharon Jennings and Mireille Levert, Annick Press, 1990. Jeremiah cannot fall asleep because his books, toys, shoes and so on are conspiring to keep him awake. One of three Jeremiah titles.

My Arctic 1, 2, 3, by Michael Kusugak and Vladyana Krykorka, Annick Press, 1996. Acclaimed Inuit storyteller Kusugak introduces readers to Arctic animals, landscape and people in a counting book format.

Thomas' Snowsuit and *The Paperbag Princess*, by Robert Munsch and Michael Martchenko, Annick Press, 1985, 1980. Two of the very best from Canada's most famous author/illustrator duo. Thomas hates wearing his snowsuit; and the princess doesn't marry the prince after all.

Uncle Henry's Dinner Guests, by Benedicte Froissart and Pierre Pratt, Annick Press, 1990. Two children at a formal dinner are expected to behave. But how can they when the chickens on Uncle Henry's shirt start acting up?

Where the Wild Things Are, Maurice Sendak, Harper & Row, 1963. Many consider this the best picture book ever written. Behaving badly, a young boy is sent to his bedroom. There he enjoys a wild ride with his own temper.

Zoom at Sea, by Tim Wynne-Jones and Eric Beddows, Groundwood, 1983. The first in the Zoom books, this is the story about a very independent cat on a wonderful journey.

Don't forget three series that have stood the test of time: *Madeline*, Ludwig Bemelmans (Puffin Books); *Curious George*, Margret and H.A. Rey (Houghton Mifflin Company); and *Babar*, Jean de Brunhoff (Random House).

READING LEADS TO WRITING

If you have been raising a reader, rest assured that you have also been raising a writer. If your child loves reading books, you can be certain that your child will want to make up her own stories and put them into books. This is only natural. Reading and writing are linked together with listening and speaking – all are communication skills. Soon it will not be enough for your daughter to write her name proudly on the inside cover of a book she owns; she will want to make her own book.

Ridiculous, you say. But look at what your child has learned about language simply because you have been reading aloud to her.

- We read from left to right.
- We read from top to bottom.
- Words go in a straight line across a page.
- Words are made up of letters, some big, some small.
- Words are separated by spaces.
- Words mean something. C-a-t means that thing that purrs and meows.
- C-a-t will always mean that thing that purrs and meows. Tomorrow, c-a-t will not mean that thing that growls and barks.

When children reach this level of understanding about books, they become very keen about telling their own stories. They understand that if something has happened in their lives, they can tell about it with words and pictures, and they can share this story with others. Be prepared for this phase of development, or you may find yourself in the following scenario.

One little girl was so in love with her books and the beautiful stories they told that she decided to add to the illustrations and color all over the pages. Her mother was so angry that she put the books in a locked cupboard and told the child that only she, the mother, could touch the books. The mother believed that the child had ruined the books; the child believed that she was showing ownership and love.

What should we do in a similar situation? Well, unless the books in question are priceless heirlooms (in which case they should be brought out only for reading time), how much damage has really been done? We should never give our kids the message that books are more precious than they are, and we can encourage our children to write and illustrate their own wonderful stories.

Your child has probably gone through dozens of boxes of crayons and markers, thousands of pieces of paper, hundreds of coloring books, and a million or so stickers, bottles of glue, and who knows what in your quest to keep him busy and happy. Now he wants to write a book. He went to the zoo, the store, the park, and he wants to tell about it. Put a few pieces of paper together with staples, and tell him you will help him with the words after he has drawn a picture on each page. Praise the finished product. Call it a book in front of everyone and read it aloud several times. And when the child has finally lost interest in this first book, be sure to put it away in a safe place so that you can produce the masterpiece at a later date, perhaps when your child is a famous author.

Now is the time when it is very important for you to encourage your child's enthusiasm for writing. You can do this by:

- making sure your child has lots of writing supplies – paper, pencils, crayons, etc.
- buying magnetic fridge letters
- buying a felt board and/or chalkboard
- buying lots of alphabet stuff – books, blocks, placemats, posters, etc.

CHAPTER SEVEN

Your child goes off to school

You have had roughly five years to raise a child who loves books and who wants to learn to read. Now, as your child starts school, the formal expansion of his or her abilities is about to begin. As you read over the next few pages, you will understand why it is so important that you have been reading to your child. You will understand that your child, with his or her love of books, has a jump-start on the formal study of how to decode our language.

HOW THE SCHOOL EVALUATES YOUR CHILD

So what happens on that first day of school? When your child enters the classroom, the teacher will probably ask him his name. Then she'll ask him if he can pick his nametag out of the bunch on the table. You wait anxiously to see if Michael is going to embarrass you. He chooses his name with a great flourish. Then the teacher asks Michael to pick a book off the shelf and go sit with the other children on the carpet. Again you watch anxiously. When Michael shows great delight at getting to choose a favorite book, and then willingly joins the others, quietly turning the pages, both you and the teacher breathe a sigh of relief. You've been reading to Michael for years, and you are relieved the child demonstrated his great ability. The teacher is thrilled because she already knows that Michael will be an enthusiastic pupil. She also knows that you, as a parent, will be an ally, a partner in the education process.

Depending upon where you live, your child will start school between the ages of three-and-a-half and six. Your child will begin school in either junior or senior kindergarten, or, in some cases, in grade one. Every school board has a different way of evaluating your child's abilities and uses different jargon to explain the evaluation process. In general, however, the evaluation process for reading over the first two or three years of school will help you know, at any given time, whether your child is an emergent reader, a beginning reader, a developing reader or an independent reader. Each of these stages can be broken down into three parts. Does your child enjoy reading? Does your child have a knowledge of books and print? Does your child use skills and strategies to understand books and print? At this stage, the three are equally important.

1. THE EMERGENT READER

Shows that she enjoys books by:
- wanting to look at books
- eagerly listening to stories
- requesting favorite books
- participating willingly during group storytime

Shows that she has a knowledge of books and print by:
- turning pages and moving front to back
- using the pictures to help understand the story
- recognizing that books have titles
- identifying with characters or plot
- making up stories

Shows that she can use skills and strategies by:
- imitating reading
- memorizing favorite bits of story
- making personal comments about the story

2. THE BEGINNING READER

Can do all of the above, and shows that he enjoys books by:
- asking to be read to
- joining in the reading aloud of favorite books or predictable books

- beginning to read to other children
- showing an interest in his own writing
- announcing proudly, "I can read this."

Shows that he has a knowledge of books and print by:
- reading top to bottom and left to right
- pointing to words in the story
- knowing some sounds and letters
- retelling the story in his own words
- noticing things like page numbers

Shows that he can use skills and strategies by:
- using memory, pictures, repetition of words and patterns to "read"
- reading very simple stories
- recognizing familiar words: cat, dog, baby
- recognizing words like: the, a, to
- predicting the story by using pictures and guesses

3. THE DEVELOPING READER

Can do all of the above, and shows that she enjoys books by:
- choosing books based on her interests
- reading a variety of books: poetry, stories, non-fiction
- reading other children's writing

Shows that she has a knowledge of books and print by:
- discussing the story using her own words
- predicting what will happen in the story
- recognizing differences between fiction, non-fiction, and verse
- using beginning and ending sounds for sounding out
- recognizing some sound/symbol relationships ("sh" for shoe)

Shows that she can use skills and strategies by:

- reading carefully, word by word
- predicting new words using clues
- trying to sound out new words using sound/symbol relationships already learned
- rereading when the meaning isn't clear
- moving between reading aloud and reading silently

4. THE INDEPENDENT READER

Can do all of the above, and shows that he enjoys books by:

- enjoying longer story sessions
- reading with increased speed
- reading for a variety of reasons – interest, information and so on
- wanting to talk about the characters, plot, events of the book
- showing a preference for books and authors
- being confident that he is a reader

Shows that he has a knowledge of books and print by:

- referring to the different parts of a book (title, table of contents, etc.)
- talking about character, plot and so on
- understanding the need for punctuation and capitalization
- having a greater understanding of letter-sound relationships and common spelling patterns

Shows that he can use skills and strategies by:

- using a great number of language rules to figure out new words
- self-correcting if what he just read didn't make sense
- reading silently most of the time

Different evaluation programs are in effect across the country. According to the guidelines given above, some children will be classified as independent readers when they enter grade two. But other evaluation guidelines will not refer to children as independent readers until they are in the junior grades – grades four, five and six.

According to the guidelines above, you might have a book-loving child who demonstrates some of the characteristics of the independent reader even though she is just starting junior kindergarten and won't be four until November. Confusing? Of course. But our job as parents is not to get hung up on jargon and classifications and groupings. Our job at this stage is to make sure that we understand what is going on at our children's schools, how reading is being taught, and what we can continue to do to support our children.

UNDERSTANDING YOUR CHILD'S SCHOOL

Within the first few weeks of the school year, you will be invited into the school along with all the other parents to formally meet the teacher and see your child's classroom.

Make sure that you attend this meeting. This is your opportunity to become familiar with the school's programs. You will also be making a clear statement to both the teacher and your child that his education is important to you.

On Parents' Night, the teacher will talk about the year's objectives and explain how these objectives will be met. She will probably have lots of handouts that explain the school's philosophy and will give examples of the kind of work your child will be doing. By now, the teacher will most likely have some samples of your child's work to show you as well.

One of the most important issues that your teacher will discuss with you is how she will set about teaching reading. She will outline her philosophy and her methods, and she will tell you her expectations. Understanding how your child will be taught formal reading instruction is very important, and will be discussed in Chapter 8.

After the teacher has finished her introductory talk, she will invite you to look around the room, to sit at your child's desk and browse through his folder. These are the things you should look for in your child's classroom:

- Are there lots of books in different areas of the room? For example, are there science books by the fish tank and gerbil cage? Are there nature books beside the leaf and pine-cone collection? Is there a reading-cosy-corner with shelves of books from which the children can choose? Are there dictionaries, encyclopedias and other reference books?

- Does the children's artwork decorate the room in joyous confusion? Or has the teacher decorated with only her materials?
- Do you see signs of lots of ongoing projects in different stages of completion?
- Is there a computer?
- Is there a borrow-a-book program in the class?

None of these guarantees that your child will learn to read by the end of the year, but they do suggest that learning is taking place in an inspirational, enthusiastic atmosphere. They also tell you that the teacher has created a literacy environment.

Once you've taken a good look around, vowed to read over the handouts and, if necessary, come back and ask lots of questions, what else should you do on Parents' Night?

1. Tell the teacher that you are available to help out every now and then – the occasional field trip – or on a weekly basis. Some parents contribute by creating the class's monthly calendar of events on computer at home or office. Others go into the class every day and read for a few minutes with one or two children. If you work full-time, can you be available for career day?

The importance of getting into your child's classroom, even on an occasional basis, cannot be overemphasized. You will be amazed at the crises and problems that a teacher copes with every day. Parents are often quick to criticize a teacher without fully understanding her job, or without knowing how their little darling carries on with other kids. On the other hand, you may be faced with the reality that your child's teacher is neither efficient nor effective. But you will never know the situation if you don't go into the classroom.

2.   Ask the teacher what his expectations are regarding home-work. What sort of work, how much and how often will it be sent home? How does the teacher want you to help out?

3.   Ask about the classroom's use of the school library. (Let's hope that your school has a library.)

4.   Take a good look around the hallways and main office area. Are kids' projects and artwork displayed proudly throughout the school? Are there lots of photographs of children and teachers participating in school events? Such things are clues that tell you that from the principal to the custodians, this is a school that enjoys its job.

5.   Ask about joining the Parent Teacher Association (PTA), or Home and School Association (HSA).

Although you shouldn't hesitate to ask questions during Parents' Night, remember that the teacher is speaking generally to the whole group. It is unrealistic to expect her to talk individually to each parent about each child. So read through all of the information that you have been given, then phone or drop by the school and set up a personal appointment to discuss everything you want to know. Don't wait for report-card interviews to do this. These personal interviews, usually running 15 minutes, may not be enough for your needs. If you have worries, then even a couple of months may be too long to wait. Remember, you are in a partnership with your school. You pay the taxes and you have the right to talk to the school about your child's education. As long as you don't expect your child's teacher to drop everything and be immediately available the second you show up, you have every right to ask questions and get the information you need.

When you involve yourself in this way with your child's school, you are telling your child that he is important to you. You are letting him know that there is no boundary between home and school, that learning happens in both places and both places are connected. By the way: you have until grade six to be part of your child's school day. Up until then, your child will be thrilled to know that Mommy or Daddy is coming to school today. After that, your child will die of mortification if you get within 10 metres of him in the school area.

CHAPTER EIGHT

How does the school teach your child to read?

Every teacher, every school, every school board and every teachers' college has a different idea about the best way to teach a child to read. Hundreds of books have been written about the success or failure of all the various systems. Some schools believe that phonics is the only way to go; other schools have virtually banned phonics outright. Some teachers believe in reading aloud to pupils every day – a whole language strategy; other teachers have been told that their jobs are on the line if they continue wasting their pupils' time by reading aloud. Some teachers swear by basal readers; others won't tolerate them in the classroom.

The truth is that a good teacher wants your child to learn how to read. A good teacher knows that children learn to read in a variety of ways, and so will use every approach, every method and strategy necessary to make your child an eager and competent reader. These include phonics *and* whole language strategies.

UNDERSTANDING SCHOOL TERMINOLOGY

Basal Readers For years, almost every child in North America has used a basal system for reading instruction. Publishers spend millions of dollars in research and development to create a series of graded textbooks, workbooks, skills books, tests, evaluation guidelines, teacher's guides and other materials for use in the elementary grades. Basal systems are used because they provide a carefully structured, step-by-step approach to teaching reading. Initially, these basal readers will introduce phonics rules. From grade three on, they develop more word-attack, spelling and comprehension skills in a logical – though perhaps artificial – sequence. With each new unit, the books become more difficult. Those who do not like basal readers point to the infamous Dick and Jane books, but the basal series produced in the last few years do not bear the least resemblance to those boring and artificial readers. Now the texts use wonderfully creative and imaginative stories, multicultural offerings, a much larger vocabulary, different types of writing – poems, cartoons, riddles and so on – and the artwork in the books is truly first class.

Phonics This is the process by which children learn to associate letters and groups of letters with specific sounds. Once a child has learned certain rules and certain sounds, she is supposed to be able to sound out new words. Phonics begins in kindergarten with the teaching of the alphabet and first letter sounds, "C" is for cat, for example. The work will be reinforced through songs and stories. In grade one, lessons will be reinforced with many worksheets – "seatwork," as it's called. Of course, being able to sound out a new word doesn't mean the child can understand the word. To equate reading with simply being able to sound out any new word is the same as suggesting that, as adults, we can understand a foreign language if we can sound out the words. Over the years, too many teachers believed that they had taught their pupils to read if they had drilled them well in phonics. This problem led to the whole language movement.

Whole Language Proponents of the whole language philosophy believe that basal readers, skills sheets, workbooks and so on fragment the language and make it meaningless. They see such a step-by-step approach as artificial and arbitrary. They believe that children learn to read because they are driven to make meaning, to understand and make sense of their lives. They see basal readers as doing nothing but killing a child's natural enthusiasm for reading. They believe a classroom should be filled with all kinds of reading material, and that each child, choosing a story or magazine or newspaper or whatever, will learn to read because he or she wants to. Those who turn purple with rage when discussing this philosophy maintain that whole language enthusiasts believe that a child will learn to read by osmosis. The irony in this debate is that in the last few years, the basal readers being produced have been heavily influenced by whole language movement gurus.

Child-centered Originally, the concept referred to the fact that the child should always be the focus of any education system, and that enjoyment and a sense of accomplishment should accompany the learning opportunity. Now, however, many people take this expression to mean that a child should never be criticized or failed in case it destroys her self-esteem.

Look-say (or Sight Recognition) The look-say approach refers to teaching through memorization of common words, rather than phonics (sounding out). "Is," "the," "of," "are" and "am" are a few of the 200 or so words that can be taught in this way. These words are beyond the phonic capabilities of young children, and yet are necessary if children are going to read meaningful, interesting stories, and not such artificially stilted lines of text as "Look! Look! See Dick run. See Jane run." These frequently used sight words are taught through much repetition in class. Critics of look-say note that many teachers teach every word using this method, and that reading becomes a matter of guesswork as children try to remember if they have been shown a particular word before.

Structural Analysis The structural analysis approach teaches children about suffixes, prefixes, compound words and contractions. Years ago, basal readers would not have used any of the above constructions – for example, the contraction "don't" – in a story because it would have been judged too difficult a concept for a grade-one child. But whole language philosophy maintains that if a child can use a word in everyday language, then a child is capable of understanding it in written language.

Context This strategy teaches a child to look for clues about a word's meaning in the rest of the sentence and in the accompanying illustration. If a child comes across the word "dinosaur" in a sentence, he may initially have a problem. Three syllables and the sophisticated "aur" ending looks a little overwhelming. But perhaps there is a picture in the story that will help, or perhaps the story has already mentioned such words as museum, bones, dig. Something will give the child the clue he needs and suddenly the word "dinosaur" will pop out of his mouth like magic. Dick and Jane never encountered dinosaurs because it was believed the word was too complicated for six-year-olds. But today's six-year-olds are immersed in dinosaur culture and demand to use such words in their own written stories.

Invented Spelling This refers to the way a child will spell a word she wants to use in a story even if she doesn't know the correct spelling. Using what she knows of phonics, she will sound out the word and "invent" a spelling that will move her along in her writing. Usually, she will be able to read the word correctly when she rereads her story aloud to the teacher. Teachers encourage invented spelling in the early grades because it demonstrates a child's willingness to take risks with the sounds she does know. Teachers also encourage this method because if children were only allowed to use words in their writing that they can spell, their stories would be very boring indeed. Parents have a hard time with the idea of invented spelling because they think every word a child uses should be corrected immediately. Instead of seeing that their child took a chance on "skeleton" – "scaltn" – they see a mistake. Critics of invented spelling believe that a child who has been taught phonics rarely makes spelling guesses.

HOW IS READING TAUGHT?

 Reading instruction is divided into two parts: word-attack skills and comprehension skills. Word-attack skills help with *decoding* our complex language; comprehension is *understanding* the meaning of the word.

Word-attack skills enable a child to decode words, which is necessary before comprehension can take place. But comprehension doesn't automatically follow just because the child can sound out the words. Many children will read a sentence fluently and not understand what it means. "Jim had a dog, but it ran away" seems like a straightforward statement, and one easily read by a child of six. But does the child understand the significance of "had" and "but"? Does the child understand that the word "it" refers to the dog? Many children do not. Asked to paraphrase, they might ask you if Jim has a dog. They have only understood "Jim" and "dog." If you point to "ran away," they understand that dogs run. These children do not comprehend because they don't understand verb tense, cause and effect, nor the subtle nuances of our language – "ran away" has a meaning beyond the literal one.

All of us have probably had the experience of hearing someone tell a joke in a foreign language. Someone decides to translate for us and does a great job until the punchline. Then she stops: "Oh, sorry. This bit doesn't translate well. It's not funny in English." The same thing happens to the child who lacks comprehension skills – nothing translates well; the words don't mean what they should.

It is fairly easy for teachers to teach your child decoding skills. They do this by teaching phonics, by teaching the look-say words, structural analysis and context skills. But how can they teach comprehension? The best way is by having a read-aloud storytime each day and by discussing the story with the children. A teacher does this by announcing that he is going to read a particular book, for example, Rhea Tregebov's *The Big Storm*. He holds up the book and

45

asks the children what they think the story will be about. The cover shows a little girl holding a cat in a snowstorm. The children will offer up all kinds of ideas, and they will also add in some experiences of their own. "I have a cat!" "Me too!" "I like snow." "Me too." And so on. "Ahh," says the teacher, "but do cats like snow?" After some more heated discussion, the teacher begins the story.

What is the point of this talk, you ask? The teacher has brought the kids into a state of comprehension readiness. Their thoughts are focused on the story and they are bringing their own experiences and knowledge to the story as it is being read. Children need to make connections between what they already know and the new material they are about to encounter if they are to make meaning. Experts often use the term "scaffolding" to explain how to get from a known piece of information to the new piece of information to be learned.

The story begins "Once upon a time, there was a little girl called Jeanette and a cat name Kitty Doyle. Jeanette and Kitty Doyle lived above the delicatessen, where every morning was a busy morning." Now the teacher asks, "Is this going to be a fairy tale?" The children discuss the opening phrase "once upon a time." But there are no delicatessens in fairy tales, some children will claim. "What is a delicatessen?" and the children will be off again, sharing their information and experiences.

And so the session will continue, the teacher asking questions, the children commenting on all the details of the story and pictures. The teacher is teaching the children that stories are about something and must be understood and interpreted. Stories are not just words to be sounded out.

When the story has been read, the teacher may further develop comprehension skills by giving the children some seatwork. He may hand out a sheet of questions about the story that ask for some specific details about the events, the order in which the events took place, as well as about the main idea or topic of the story. He may also ask the children to retell the story in their own words. An excellent activity at any grade level is to ask the children to make up their own stories based on the events of the story just read.

Not all teachers are good at teaching comprehensions skills. Many of them do not take their pupils through a story by modeling, or showing the pupils their own thought process as they work through a story. In *The Big Storm,* the teacher would probably stop when he came to the part where Jeanette realizes her cat is waiting for her outside in the snowstorm. "How could she have forgotten? Kitty Doyle would never have forgotten about her." The teacher would ask his students if such a thing has ever happened to them. How did they feel? How do they think Jeanette feels? What do they think will happen next? He would probably add in something about his own experiences and thoughts.

Unfortunately, many teachers do not realize the importance of approaching a story in this way. They use storytime as a way to quiet down an unruly class, or as a filler for the few minutes before hometime.

 It is easy for you, as a parent, to teach comprehension skills. You have been doing just that by reading aloud to your child since she was born. You have been surrounding her with language, drenching her with the subtleties and sophistication of the written word. Your child has absorbed the complexities of language in a way that is almost impossible to understand. She has demonstrated her comprehension of a story every time she asks you a question about it, every time she paraphrases the story or relates aspects of the story to her own life.

Tips for encouraging reading comprehension at home

1. Continue reading together each day, taking turns reading aloud.

2. Read a wide variety of materials – stories, poems, riddles, jokes, comics, magazines, scientific books, historical non-fiction and so on.

3. Read books beyond your child's reading ability.

4. Tell your child what you think about the story as you go.

5. Ask your child what he thinks about the story.

6. Ask your child some "why" questions about the story. Why did the author say this? Why did the illustrator show this?

7. Encourage your child to take risks with an unknown word. Don't criticize a wrong decision. Emphasize the need to make sense.

8. Encourage your child to write her own stories. Use a story that has been read together to inspire the child.

9. Discuss differences between a book and a movie that has been adapted from the book.

10. Discuss the books written by a favorite author. Are they alike? Why or why not?

11. Ask your child to read to a younger child. Encourage your child to play teacher with the younger child.

CHAPTER NINE

Fawnix, ghonyks, phonics

Many educators feel that parents should leave the word-attack skills to the school – this is *work*, after all – and concentrate on developing their child's comprehension skills – the *fun* stuff. But many parents, faced with children who are reading, writing and spelling poorly in grades two and three, start to panic. We realize that our children can't sound out anything and will give us a glazed look when we suggest this strategy for a new word.

Phonics, as we've seen, is one of the first word-attack skills. Learning the rules of phonics gives children one method of decoding words and sounding them out. Only 65 percent of English words can be decoded using the rules of phonics; the other 35 percent are exceptions, and need further rules or help from context. Some methods of teaching phonics offer up to 240 phonic bits to be learned, with up to 120 different rules for blending the bits together. Furthermore, the rules are only applicable 30 to 70 percent of the time.

Although most of us have probably been doing a bit of simple phonics since day one – "Yes, Cathy, 'cat' begins with the letter c just like your name." – we decide to move into more complicated work.

With this chapter's title, we've had some fun with the word "phonics" itself. The "ph" sound can be an "f," but it can also be "gh" as in cough. The "o" can be "aw" if you're from the Prairies. The "i" can by a "y," and the "cs" can be "ks" or simply "x." You can see why teaching a child the rules of letter-sound relationships is not a task to be undertaken lightly.

There are many books and packages on the market which will help you teach your child phonics at home. Most bookstores carry a series of graded reading readiness and spelling workbooks that cost around three or four dollars each, and there may be several manuals per grade level. Some books are available that cost between fifty and sixty dollars. And, of course, there are phonics kits you can order that carry a hefty price tag. In general, whatever program you choose, you will be guided to teach your child the rules in the following order:

1. the five short vowel sounds - "c<u>a</u>t," but not "<u>ate</u>"
2. all consonants spelled by single letters - "<u>at</u>," but not "<u>ch</u>urch"
3. consonants and consonant combinations spelled with two or three letters - "lu<u>ck</u>" and "du<u>mp</u>" or "pa<u>nts</u>"
4. vowels and vowel combinations spelled with two letters - "b<u>ee</u>," "<u>ea</u>ch"
5. the five long vowels - "n<u>a</u>me," "k<u>i</u>te"
6. irregular spellings - "knife," "steak," "bread," "cough"
7. all sorts of rules will be interspersed with these lessons - the doubling up of consonants - "ho<u>pp</u>ed"; the difference between hopped and hoped; the different ways to make plurals - pony becomes ponies, but horse becomes horses; and so on.

Depending upon the phonics package you purchase, you may or may not be introduced to the more sophisticated terms during the above lessons: digraphs (special two-letter combinations like "ch," "ng," "qu"; diphthongs (vowel combinations like "oo," "ay," "ea"; phonograms (special combinations like "ight," "tion"; or blends (letter combinations that must be blended together like "pl," "nk," "str."

However the information is presented, the lessons will be set out using materials similar to the seatwork handed out in your child's classroom. For example, a picture of a cat and an apple will be drawn above the word "cat" and "apple," beside a small and capital letter "a." Then there will be a list of words, with an accompanying picture, that use the short "a" sound. Your child fills in the vowel. H_t, m_t, s_t and so on.

There will be a lesson for each short-vowel sound, and you will be encouraged to go over each lesson several times. You will be warned about letting your child guess at a word, and it will be suggested that you go back a few lessons if your child is guessing too often.

As you can see, undertaking a phonics course at home is not for the faint of heart. It requires quite a commitment on your part. And, because you are doing more classroom work at home, be prepared to meet with some resistance from your child.

If you decide to start a home phonics program:

- Do not forego the nightly read-aloud session in favor of more word-attack skills.
- Do not focus on your child's inabilities. Focus on what he gets right.
- Don't begin the skills work the moment your child gets home from school. Give her a break between school and home.
- Don't do too much work each day. One lesson page is probably enough.

There are several other points that you should consider along with a home-teaching program.

- Have you discussed your concerns with your child's teacher?
- Is it possible for your child's teacher to send some work home for you and your child to work on together that will reinforce what is being taught at school?
- Are you reading with your child each day?
- Do you point out interesting and unusual words in whatever story you are reading? Do you discuss why this word is spelled this way?
- Do you point out words in the environment as often as possible – "exit," "stop," "do not enter" and so on?

- Do you leave notes around that are easy (and meaningful) for your child to read? For example, "The cookies are in the cookie jar."
- Do you play games in the car, looking for signs, license plates and so on?
- Do you share your own writing with your child? Show him a note or letter you are writing?
- Does your child have lots of writing materials?
- Do you get your child to make birthday cards and thank-you cards?
- Do you always praise your child's efforts at spelling? Remember to praise what she gets right, not criticize what she gets wrong.
- Have you bought your child a picture dictionary?
- Have you bought your child some simple crossword puzzles or word games such as Scrabble?

As mentioned in other sections of *Raising a Reader*, educators either love or hate phonics, and you may or may not be encouraged by your child's teacher to pursue a phonics course at home. But consider this parent's story. "My oldest child did not start reading until he was in grade four. That was when he received remedial attention and, after three months of phonics for an hour a day, he had surpassed his classmates in reading ability. Absolutely, this child needed the structure of phonics to succeed. But I have two other children. They were both reading halfway through grade one, and it came to them as naturally as breathing."

Just remember: do not teach phonics in place of reading aloud to your child. Continue reading aloud daily, and make sure that the books are exciting and interesting to your child. This will reinforce the connection between the phonics work – decoding the language – and the ability to read wonderful stories.

CHAPTER TEN

ABC:
Grades One, Two, Three

School can be a hit-or-miss affair. Your child may adapt wonderfully and love going off to school each day. Or he may be extremely shy and find himself overwhelmed by the structure of school and by all the other children. Or she may be bored to tears with the lessons and the repetition and the rules. Your job is to be there at the end of the day and somehow put the whole learning scenario into perspective.

 While your child is grappling with the school experience of learning how to read, reading aloud with you sustains the comfortable, intimate and pleasurable experience of books. Reading aloud with your son reminds him that everything he is doing at school has a purpose. Reading aloud with your daughter motivates her to do well in class.

HOW TO KEEP READING SPECIAL AT HOME

1. Read aloud to your child every day for pleasure. Don't turn this time together into a school lesson.
2. If possible, read stories that you read as a child. Share any memories that come up as you read these old favorites. Did you want to go to convent school with Madeline? Did you wish you owned a monkey named Curious George?

3.	Make sure that your child has a library card. If not, go to your local library as soon as possible and sign up. Ask the librarian to show you around the children's section and teach your child how to choose books. Find out if your library has programs for kids. Pick a day that you and your child can go to the library on a regular basis. And if *you* do not have a library card, now is the time to get one. Make going to the library a family event.

4.	Set up a bookshelf in your child's bedroom and start collecting books. Ownership of a favorite book is a very special feeling. Ask for books for gifts; buy as many books as you can afford; look for books in garage sales, rummage sales, used book stores. Take advantage of the deals offered through school book clubs and fairs.

5.	Install a reading lamp in your child's bedroom. Tell your child that he or she is allowed to stay up a bit longer as long as he or she is reading in bed. This has a threefold benefit – it cuts down on the arguments over bedtime; it gives your child a tremendous sense of empowerment; it gives reading a special status.

READING ALOUD WITH THE SCHOOL-AGE CHILD

Once your child has started school, there are two appoaches to reading aloud. First, there are the books your child will try to read aloud herself and, second, there are the more difficult books that you will read aloud to your child.

When Your Child Reads to You

Fairly soon after your child starts school, he should be coming home with books that he has chosen from the library or from his classroom's borrow-a-book program. If he has received guidance from the librarian or teacher, then the books will have:

•	simple vocabulary and short sentences
•	not too many words on each page
•	lots of illustrations that match the text of the story and give clues about unknown words
•	repetition of words or sentences
•	large type

You may be surprised to note that a number of the books that your child brings home are books that you read to him when he was three or four years old. Don't worry. Your child is not beyond these books, nor is the reading program at your school too easy. These books are once again suitable for your child because he can now read them himself. He will feel comforted to come across familiar stories, and he will be proud that he can now read stories that only Mommy or Daddy could read before. But whatever book your child brings home, rest assured that he will be very keen to show off his new-found expertise. He will want you to sit beside him and listen as he demonstrates his ability to read some words straight off and to sound out unfamiliar ones.

As your child progresses through the first three grades of school, her word-attack skills will increase, and she will bring home more sophisticated and complex books. She will begin to choose books that reflect her interests and offer her information about her world. You will notice that these books have:

- longer sentences and more difficult words, for example, "Wild geese come calling up the wind and crocuses break through the brown grasses, and soon, as the ground begins to dry on the southern coulee slopes, dry malongo appears." (*Tess*, by Hazel Hutchins)
- more print per page
- fewer, or smaller, illustrations
- stories about characters solving problems on their own
- stories about conflict

Whatever stage your child is at, follow these guidelines as your child reads aloud to you:

1. Remember to encourage and praise your child.
2. Don't force your child to sound out words if she is struggling.
3. Don't overcorrect your child, or call attention to each error.
4. Ask your child if he wants you to help out.
5. Suggest that you take turns reading – the "I read, you read" strategy.

Remember, your child is struggling to show you what she *does* know; she doesn't want too much attention paid to what she doesn't know. So don't say, "Oh, come on! You read that word on the last page. How come you don't remember it again now?" Say instead, "Didn't we see that word someplace before? Hmmm. Let's have a look. Oh, here it is. See – r-a-b-b-i-t. Do you remember now? And see, here's a picture to help."

If your child is stumbling over too many words, chances are the book is too difficult and both you and your child will feel mounting frustration. Teachers use the five-finger reading check to tell if a book is beyond a child. Without letting your child see, curl up one finger with each error or stumble your child makes. If all five fingers are curled up by the end of a page, you will know that the book is too hard. Say to your child, "Wow! This book is really tricky. Do you want me to help out with it or should we pick another book?"

When You Read to Your Child

In chapter 2 we discussed the importance of reading aloud, and it has been mentioned over and over again throughout *Raising a Reader*. But when our children begin reading for themselves, we often mistakenly think that we are doing enough if we listen to them read aloud to us each night. As we have seen, however, our children may be going back and reading books that we read to them as toddlers as they master the twists and turns of the English language. So our job now is to read books to them that are beyond their reading abilities at this point. We should be reading stories and poems to them that will perhaps be stretched out over a number of nights. We can also introduce our children to books that they would not discover for themselves for a number of years – classics, mythology, folk tales. When we read aloud these more sophisticated books, we are allowing our children to understand how writers use words, how they create plots, how they use such literary devices as imagery, alliteration, symbolism and metaphor. Our children also are allowed to hear how a fluent reader sounds when reading aloud.

When a child falls in love with a book that is being read aloud to her, but is beyond her capabilities, you can be fairly certain that that child will want to read it herself one day. A goal has been set, a challenge has been offered, and you did it in the most positive way possible. Consider this man's story. "When I was six, my mother bought me Pierre Berton's just-published *The Secret World of Og*. I remember sitting in my mother's lap day after day as we read about all of Berton's children discovering the people under the playhouse. I wanted to be those children. I wanted my own playhouse with a secret trapdoor. I wanted brothers and sisters who were as neat as Pierre Berton's kids and who would go with me on adventures. We didn't live too far from the Bertons' farm, and so naturally I made my parents drive to Kleinburg so that I could try to figure out just where the story took place. And, as soon as I could read, I read *The Secret World of Og* over and over until it was falling apart. I know that a new edition was recently published, with new illustrations by one of Berton's daughters. I'm sure that it is lovely, but I refuse to look at it. I don't want to tamper with my memories of that story."

How do we analyze and explain this kind of magic? Many reading experts use words like absorption or immersion to explain the phenomenon of becoming part of a book. This means that the story has such a profound effect on us that we feel that we are part of what is happening in the story. We feel anger and sorrow and fear right along with the characters. We work ourselves up to indignation on behalf of the hero, and feel pride when something works out well. We rejoice in a happy ending, or feel depressed and let down with a sad conclusion. As an example of this, one woman said that no matter how many times she rereads *Gone with the Wind*, she always believes that *this* time, Rhett will not walk out.

This immersion happens for both children and adults alike. And as adults, we don't have to be reading a great book to feel pulled into the story. We can be reading one of those throwaway spy thrillers, groaning about how badly it's written, and yet still feel gripped by parts of the story. So if it isn't necessarily the quality of the book that pulls us in, that absorbs us, what does?

Experts believe that the ability to be immersed in a story is a characteristic of a good reader. A good reader, an enthusiastic reader, willingly allows the immersion to take place, willingly leaves the real world behind to enter the world of the story.

When we read aloud to our children, we set the stage for this immersion to take place. We present them with worlds and adventures, people and events that are not part of the every day. We ask them to envision the stories in their imagination and we ask them to comment on the stories as if they were real. Our children soon want to do this for themselves. They don't want to wait for Mom or Dad to have time to read: they want to open a book and be transported to the magic on their own.

As well as giving our children the gift of being able to immerse oneself in a story, there is yet another benefit to reading aloud books beyond our children's abilities: we provide them with information about people, places, events and so on, that would not be readily available to them in any other way. And information gleaned through story tends to "stick." A boy who has heard several folk tales from other countries will sit up in class when social studies are being discussed and volunteer all of his knowledge. A girl who has heard stories about whales will perk up in nature studies and demand to share what she knows. These are the children who feel confident at school and know that they are scholars. These are the children who want to read more because they like knowing what they know. These are the children who want to read harder, more sophisticated books because they like the confidence knowledge gives them.

SOME FAVORITES FOR BEGINNING READERS

Alexander and the Terrible, Horrible, No Good, Very Bad Day, by Judith Viorst and Ray Cruz, Atheneum, 1972. Every child (and adult) sympathizes with poor old Alexander who has a bad day from morning till night.

Angel Tree, by Robin Muller, Doubleday Canada, 1997. Lavish illustrations by the author accompany the spellbinding tale of young Kit, a blacksmith apprentice who is asked by an angel to save a dying tree.

The Big Storm, by Rhea Tregebov and Maryann Kovalski, Kids Can Press, 1992. The little cat Kitty Doyle always waits for Jeanette on the corner across from the school. But one snowy day, Jeanette forgets all about Kitty Doyle.

Bone Button Borscht, by Aubrey Davis and Dusan Petricic, Kids Can Press, 1995. In this wonderful retelling of a classic tale, a beggar teaches poor villagers what can be accomplished with a little co-operation.

Boy Soup, or, When Giant Caught Cold, by Loris Lesynski, Annick Press, 1996. Several children find a way to avoid being consumed as part of a giant's cold remedy. Children laugh out loud at this zany poem.

Dr. Zed's Science Surprises, by Gordon Penrose, Greey de Pencier, 1989. A fun-filled book with more than just stories.

The Ice Cream Store, by Dennis Lee and David McPhail, HarperCollins, 1991. A wonderful collection of poems that calls forth lots of giggles. For example, "Mrs. Mitchell's underwear is dancing on the line...."

Mary of Mile 18, by Ann Blades, Tundra, 1971. This charming story of Mary and her longing to keep a wolf-pup became an overnight publishing sensation. It is a definite Canadian classic with stunning illustrations by the author.

The Orphan Boy, by Tololwa M. Mollel and Paul Morin, Oxford University Press, 1990. To the Maasai in Africa, the planet Venus is known as kileken, the orphan boy. And one day, an old man is delighted to welcome a mysterious orphan boy into his childless life.

Tess, by Hazel Hutchins and Ruth Ohi, Annick Press, 1995. Tess earns a neighbor's respect when her courage saves his dog from coyotes.

The Very Last First Time, by Jan Andrews and Ian Wallace, Groundwood, 1985. When the tide goes out, a young Inuit girl is allowed to collect the mussels for the first time on her own.

The Wonderful Pigs of Jillian Jiggs, by Phoebe Gilman, Scholastic, 1988. Children love the message and the rhythm of this book. "Jillian, Jillian, Jillian Jiggs. It looks like your room has been lived in by pigs!" Jillian is now so popular that there are several other titles.

CHAPTER ELEVEN

The Grade Four turning point

By the time your child is in grade four, you will probably have heard the following expression: "In the first three grades, our children learn to read. From grade four on, our children read to learn." Although experts quibble over this statement (even a two-year-old wants to learn about himself when reading about bathtime), they generally agree that it is accurate when it comes to how schools view reading. In grade four, teachers expect that children know how to read, and the time allotted to reading instruction drops. Children begin studying the content subjects – history, science, geography – in a serious way. Teachers expect students to be able to handle the textbooks, go to the library and research materials for projects.

By grade four, most children have a minimum reading vocabulary of around 3,000 words and are able to read at least 70 words a minute. Anything less indicates that your child is struggling with decoding the language and is not reading for comprehension. How can your daughter learn about your town's history when she is still sounding out several words per paragraph in a social studies textbook? How can your son research a project on bugs when he has understood only a little of the information that he's read? Students who are having trouble are usually sent out of the classroom for special instruction. Not only do these students have a problem reading, they will now miss out on some of the material being taught in regular class.

Let's assume that your child has progressed confidently through the primary grades and is a fluent and competent reader. You breathe a sigh of relief knowing that your child will be able to handle the workload of the junior grades. Unfortunately, even good readers can run into a problem in grade four. This problem is called by many reading experts the fourth grade slump, and it refers to the sudden lack of interest your child has in reading. "Reading is boring. I hate reading," your child announces one day.

This slump is a serious problem. Ironically, it usually happens with children who can read very well. Therefore, parents and teachers often refer to it as a phase and may not take the proper steps to combat the slump. If your child isn't encouraged to read for enjoyment, then he will not progress beyond his grade-four abilities. He will enter senior school with very limited comprehension skills and vocabulary, and he will fall behind his peers. The following list provides you with some reasons for the slump:

- Reading instruction changes in the junior grades, and this often results in the teacher spending less time reading out loud to the class for enjoyment.
- At home, you may have been lulled into a false sense of security – knowing that your child can read well – and have let your regular reading sessions fall by the wayside.
- Your child, who has become a very independent young person, has dozens of other ways to occupy her time. Friends, hobbies, lessons, television and, of course, regular schoolwork all compete for the few available hours in the day.

Although it is next to impossible to change what is happening in the classroom, you are capable of changing your home environment. Quite simply, you must become involved again with your child's reading habits. You must take a look at your own commitment to reading and see, as you did in Chapter 1: Creating Fertile Ground, if reading is important in your life.

WAYS TO GET YOUR CHILD OUT OF A SLUMP

- Remember to model good reading behavior yourself. Let your child see that reading is important to you. Make sure that your child frequently sees you reading for both enjoyment and information. Make sure that your home is print-rich with newspapers, magazines and books.

- Let your child see you relaxing with a book. Tell your child that some nights you'd rather read than watch television.

- Review your child's day and week to see how free time is allotted. Are you packing too many lessons into a week? Is there too much time being spent in front of the television? Does your child talk on the phone to all 20 friends every evening? Make certain that there is time given to reading, even if you have to unplug the TV and stereo and ban all friends and phone calls.

- If you've let the reading together sessions drop, start them up again. Choose a time that works and stick to it.

- Tell your child why you are worried. Let your child know that reading is important to you. One parent said that when her son told her "I already know how to read," she replied, "Yes, and you already know how to play hockey. But when you're 12, you don't want to be playing hockey the way you do now at nine. You have to practice both hockey and reading to keep getting better."

- If your child wants nothing to do with these sessions – "This is for babies" – don't insist that your child read to you. Tell your child that you will do the reading. Pick a long chapter book beyond your child's reading skills, and read aloud every night.

- Make sure you are reading something that will interest your child. Find out what his or her friends are reading, or ask for advice from a teacher, librarian or bookstore staff. Think about what books your child has liked in the past, and keep in mind favorite hobbies or interests.

- If you've stopped visiting the library, start going again. Pick a day that works and go every one or two weeks. If possible, make this a special outing by stopping at the local hamburger joint or ice-cream parlor.

- If you can afford it, start giving your child some money once or twice a month to purchase a book. An excursion to one of the new state-of-the-art bookstores can be a real treat. Many of these stores are hooked up with coffee shops so that, after you and your child have bought books, both of you can relax over your cappuccino and hot chocolate and start reading immediately.

- Take your child to as many book events as possible. In the last few years, there has been an upswing in book fairs and writing festivals all across the country. Check out your local newspapers to find out if authors and illustrators will be appearing in your area.

- Finally, remember to work with your child's teacher. Let the teacher know that you are worried, and ask for advice.

Best Books for Developing Readers
What to Look For

- books with short chapters and a few illustrations
- greater length to the stories so that the book is read over a few days
- books in a series (Kids love to get hooked onto a character and follow him or her through many adventures.)
- books with humorous exaggeration
- stories about conflict, with heros your child's age actively solving problems
- books about mysteries, supernatural thrillers and science fiction
- informational books about any subject your child is interested in
- books of trivia and unusual facts
- books set in other times and places
- stories that begin quickly, with a conflict or problem introduced on the first page

SOME FAVORITES FOR DEVELOPING READERS

Charlotte's Web, by E.B. White, Harper & Row, 1952. No parent can ever get through this warm, wonderful story about Charlotte the spider and Wilbur the pig without crying.

The Cremation of Sam McGee, by Robert W. Service and Ted Harrison, Kids Can Press, 1986. Harrison's striking illustrations bring new life to this classic Canadian poem.

Friendship Bracelets, by Camilla Gryski, Kids Can Press, 1992. Kids will spend hours pouring over easy-to-understand directions for making bracelets. As well, check out *Cat's Cradle, Owl's Eyes: A Book of String Games*.

The Hockey Sweater, by Roch Carrier, Tundra, 1984. The very funny tale of a young boy in Montreal who receives a Toronto Maple Leaf jersey by mistake.

How Come the Best Clues Are Always in the Garbage? by Linda Bailey, Kids Can Press, 1992. This is the first book in the Stevie Diamond series. Kids love reading about the true-to-life hero who solves mysteries on her own.

Lost and Found, by Jean Little, Penguin, 1985. A girl finds a stray dog and learns about love, loneliness and responsibility.

Maggie and Me, by Ted Staunton, Kids Can Press, 1986. Maggie and Cyril can't seem to avoid trouble in this funny, touching story.

Tales of a Fourth Grade Nothing, by Judy Blume, Dell, 1972. The hero must put up with the tribulations of school and a two-year-old brother.

That Scatterbrain Booky, by Bernice Thurman Hunter, Scholastic, 1981. The author draws on her own reminiscences of growing up during wars and depression to create a charming and delightful story. Other titles include: *With Love from Booky* and *As Ever, Booky*.

There's a Snake in My Toilet, by Gisela Sherman, Minstrel Books, 1995. Ten-year-old Ollie, who is afraid of snakes, can't believe his eyes when he sees a boa constrictor coming out of his toilet.

"Boys'" books and "girls'" books

Around this age, kids tend to gravitate to books for boys or books for girls, and very often, wind up devouring series books. Boys might collect dozens of *Goosebumps*, while the girls are reaching for *The Babysitter's Club*. This is not much different than what we did at the same age, reading either *The Hardy Boys* or *Nancy Drew*. There is nothing wrong with children going through whole series of mediocre books, as long as they don't stagnate at this level. But be reassured: your child will zip through as many titles as possible thus ensuring fluency and speed.

CHAPTER TWELVE

When something goes wrong

Throughout grade one, you've been watching your child begin to master certain skills. You've seen his written stories, admired his invented spelling and his accompanying illustrations. You've listened as he has made an attempt to read simple books. His report card notes that he is in the beginning reading stage, and that he is progressing slowly, but steadily. But it is clear to you that, at the end of grade one, your child cannot read. What do you do?

Consider one mother's story. "At the end of grade one, my son could not read. His teacher said that he was such a bright little boy, reading will come soon. Don't worry. But in grade two, his new teacher called us in for an interview. She was very worried, and so were we. We had always read to our son, he had a huge book collection, and he loved books and being read aloud to very much. So what was the problem? The grade-two teacher recommended that we have him assessed. That was in September. We went on a waiting list, during which time we were told to have his hearing and vision checked. He was assessed in February, and we were called in for an interview in May. We sat in the office with the principal, the teacher, the board psychologist, the board social worker and the reading clinician who had administered the testing. The meeting lasted 10 minutes. Everyone agreed that our son couldn't read, should be reading, and needed extra help, which would begin in September.

"But in September, we found out there were no funds for extra help. Our son went on a waiting list for the board's reading clinic. We also found out that our son could be bused to a school with space. He might have to travel an hour each way on a board-funded bus for one hour of reading clinic each day. He'd lose three hours of regular school a day. And to make it really ridiculous, the bus he travelled on might have only him as a passenger – a private bus, in other words! The board would do this, but not hire another reading specialist.

"We began a letter-writing campaign and managed to catch the interest of our school trustee, who found out that several other kids in our school were also on the waiting list. Somehow, money was found to hire another specialist, and, in November, our son started a year of reading clinic in his own school. In three months, he went from reading at a preprimer level to grade level. In May we were called in for another meeting and informed that our son wouldn't need a full year's worth of clinic. But fearing that our son might lose some skills over the summer, we insisted that he stay in the clinic until his full year was up in November.

"I should also mention that for most of two years, many people suggested that we were the problem, that my husband and I didn't do enough to help our son learn to read. When I told people that I was a writer, and that my son had always been surrounded by books, these same fools then suggested that I had pushed my son too hard and this was his way of rebelling. I add in this bit because parents have to know that when something goes wrong, there will always be those who will blame them."

This woman's son was very lucky, not only because the problem was dealt with successfully, but because the child did become a good reader. Other children are not so lucky. Other children have reading disabilities that cannot be solved in a few months, or even in a few years.

If you are not satisfied with your child's progress in reading at the end of grade one, do not wait to discuss your concerns. There may, in fact, be nothing to worry about. Children progress at different speeds in reading just as they do in toilet training, walking and speaking. Usually, within the three primary grades – grades one, two, and three – children catch up to one another. But if your teacher cannot convince you that your expectations are too high and that, in fact, your child is at grade level, do not wait to seek help for your child. Request a meeting with the teacher and principal, and find out what guidance they can offer. Ask that your child be assessed by the school board. If this is impossible (location, funds, whatever) you may have to pay to have your child assessed independently.

WHY SOME CHILDREN CAN'T READ

Home Environment If your child comes from a troubled home, if there has recently been a divorce, a death, if there is constant fighting between spouses or between parents and children, your child will suffer in school. If your child does not receive adequate sleep and food, your child will suffer in school. If you show little interest in your child and her world, she will suffer in school. A five-year-old may not be able to voice her concerns about a disruptive home life, but she will show attention-seeking behavior in school and an inability to concentrate.

Does your child:

- have a comfortable and secure home environment?
- receive nutritious meals and adequate sleep?
- have a life overscheduled with too many lessons and hobbies?
- get any quiet time to be alone, to read, to think?
- watch too much television?
- get read to every day?

Sometimes we are ambushed by situations beyond our control, for example, a single parent who must work a late shift and who does not have adequate child care in the evenings, or an illness that disrupts routines. But if your child is not doing well at school, you owe it to him or her to take a long, honest look at your home environment and make any adjustments necessary.

Teachers and Schools These days our schools seem to be under siege. Governments are cutting back funds, the number of students per class is increasing in leaps and bounds, more and more children are showing up in school troubled or with special needs, and everyone, from parents to politicians, is wailing that schools aren't doing a good job. The truth is that most schools and teachers are doing an excellent job teaching our children. If any of us have any doubt about this, we should, as was suggested in Chapter 7, make sure we spend time in our child's classroom and experience a teacher's day firsthand.

And yet, if your child is not doing well at school, and you have satisfied yourself that your child has a stable and happy home life, then you must examine what is going on at the school. Hopefully, you have taken the advice offered in Chapter 7 and have become familiar with your child's teacher, classroom, principal and school. This will make it easier for you to talk about your child's performance with those concerned.

Of course there are ineffective teachers, just as there are ineffective people in all professions. Some teachers do not have any enthusiasm for their job and coast through each year. Some do not bother with a concrete, well-scheduled plan for teaching reading. Some teachers are not enthusiastic readers themselves and convey the feeling that reading is work with every lesson they teach.

But teachers don't work in a vacuum. If they are given too many children, too few materials and too little help, it will be almost impossible to teach each child well. If there isn't a school library or a nearby neighborhood library, and if funds are non-existent for interesting classroom reading materials, then how does a teacher cope? Many of our best teachers have become champion fundraisers and spend far too much of their time campaigning for materials that should be every child's right.

What can you do if you are not satisfied with your school's or teacher's performance?

1. Make sure you know your child's teacher and the school principal.
2. Talk to other parents to get their views of how their children are doing.
3. Ask for a detailed plan of how reading instruction is being taught in your child's class.
4. Ask how you can help reinforce the lesson plans at home.
5. Be on the PTA or HSA if you believe system-wide changes need to take place.

Once you have talked to your child's teacher, you may decide to offer some concrete suggestions regarding the way in which the teaching of reading is being approached in your child's class:

- Does the teacher have a detailed reading instruction plan that she can hand out to parents?
- Can the teacher offer helpful advice for work at home?
- Do the children have a class library for a borrow-a-book program? (Are you willing to start one up?)
- Do the children visit the school library and neighborhood library on a regular basis?
- Has the teacher asked parents and grandparents to come in and read one-on-one with the children?
- Will the school set up a reading-buddy system between older and younger students? (A win-win situation, by the way, because older kids love to play teacher with the little ones.)
- Would the school consider a reading-buddy system with a nearby seniors' home? (Another win-win situation.)
- Is your school aware that it can book children's writers and illustrators for school visits?
- Is your school aware of the many writing and reading contests that school-age children can enter?

Does Your Child Have a Disability?   Once you have concluded that both home and school are in great shape, you are faced with that very difficult question: What's wrong with my child? No parent wants to think that their child has a problem and yet, if all the other children in the class are doing well and your child is struggling, then you must honestly assess the needs and abilities of your child.

The label "learning disabled" strikes fear into the heart of all parents, so much so that some experts refuse to use this term, and instead use "learning difference." And, indeed, there are many children who adapt very well when they are presented with a different *style* of learning. Some children, for example, are kinetic learners – they need to move around and use their body to help them take in and store information. Others learn more effectively if they see or hear the material – visual or oral learners. These children are often misdiagnosed when it is a simple matter of how these children learn best.

By now you will have spoken to your child's teacher and possibly the principal. Hopefully, everyone is in agreement with you that your child needs help, and none of them will drag their feet. Depending upon where you live, there will be any number of experts or specialists who will assess your child.

 Do not forget to talk to your child's doctor about your concerns. He or she will give your child a physical examination, and will be able to offer advice and suggestions for you to follow. Make certain that the medical test results are analyzed in conjuction with the educational tests. Your doctor can also direct you to groups and organizations that will offer you support, guidance and information.

Theories about learning disabilities are changing constantly and vary from specialist to specialist. In general, there are three main categories: developmental deficiencies; hyperactivity; dyslexia.

Developmental Deficiencies   Growth and development, starting with conception, progress through a series of stages. If the stages of growth are disrupted or, for some reason, do not progress as they should, minimal brain damage can result. Some of the causes besides heredity are viral illnesses during pregnancy, a prolonged labor, a lack of oxygen during birth, head injuries, allergies and poisoning. In addition, if a child does not receive a lot of stimulation and encouragement during the early years, learning disabilities may result.

Dyslexia With this disability, the brain jumbles the information it receives from the child's senses. As such, it is a neurological disorder that creates a perception problem. The result is a difficulty in concentrating, in using letters and numbers, in understanding such concepts as distance and time. A child will read "d" for "b," will say "saw" instead of "was," and mix up numbers – "21" for "12." Some children have only slight problems and respond to simple therapy; other children require intensive treatment. Unfortunately, dyslexia can often go undetected and a child be labeled "slow" or "underachieving." This may make the problem worse. (A word of caution: occasionally, most young children mix up letters like "b" and "d" and words like "was" and "saw." Don't jump to conclusions because of these beginning learner mistakes.)

Hyperactivity (ADD or ADHD) It is believed that hyperactivity – which is also called Attention Deficit Disorder or Attention Deficit Hyperactivity Disorder – is the result of a combination of biochemical, metabolic, nutritional and allergy disturbances. Hyperactive children are restless, inattentive, easily excitable and often aggressive. They cannot stop moving or talking, they are impulsive and impatient, they may have sleep problems. They are often unable to play with other children and are disruptive in class.

Most parents of hyperactive children know that something is wrong by the time the child is two or three years old. If, however, nothing is done until the child reaches school, then the problem snowballs as the child is unable to fit in. Almost all hyperactive children have problems learning.

Experts believe that drug-free nutritional therapy is the answer for hyperactivity. A diet free of sugar, food colorings and chemical additives can produce dramatic behavioral results. Others point to the need for therapy to reinforce weak or non-existant developmental skills. However, many children have been prescribed the drug Ritalin, which is a stimulant. It works by stimulating the attention center in a child's brain, allowing the child to control his attention and motor activity. He appears quieter and more attentive because he is in better control of himself. But a controversy exists regarding the prescribing of drugs for children. Many children do not respond to the medication, and some require higher and higher doses to remain stable. As well, there are often side effects such as loss of appetite and "rebound irritability" – as the medication wears off, the child seems even more restless. In a few cases, tics affecting the voice and body have developed. Should your child be prescribed Ritalin, you must monitor his health constantly in order to give your doctor the necessary feedback.

Unfortunately, a number of problems do not show up until the child enters school. That is when we notice our child's inability to master the skills of reading, writing, spelling and mathematics. That is when we begin comparing our child's behavior to the "normal" behavior of the other children and realize that our child is poorly co-ordinated, inattentive and restless. Fortunately, however, many disabilities can be helped or completely corrected. It may take a team of doctors, psychologists, social workers, teachers and any number of other specialists but, eventually, an educational package will be put together for your child. Accept nothing less.

CHAPTER THIRTEEN

Independence Day

Congratulations! You are the parent of a preteen who can not only read well, but also loves to read. Now what? Is your job over? Can you breathe a sigh of relief and feel confident about the future? As your son or daughter would say, "As if!"

The next few years are going to be very turbulent. Already, you have probably noticed the signs of hormones kicking in: the odd blemish; the occasional bit of "attitude"; changing eating and sleeping patterns; a new interest in clothes and hair; a new appreciation of the opposite sex.

Your child is also becoming more independent. She makes plans after school and phones you from her friend's house. He gets a paper route and can't make it to family events – a sibling's hockey game, for example – that he always attended before. Your daughter signs up for the school band, volleyball team and the cross-country ski team. Boy/girl parties are becoming more and more popular and, afterwards, the phone will ring constantly as your child discusses with all of his friends what everyone said and what it meant. Going to movies in large groups is a "must" in order for your child to be part of the in-crowd. Meanwhile, teachers are assigning more and more homework, and your child seems to have less and less time to get it done. Where does reading for pleasure fit into this hectic schedule?

If your child has been an enthusiastic reader up till now, he or she will probably emerge a reader on the other side of the teenage years. But you must still remain a good influence and a strong champion of reading and books over the next little while. Even a proficient reader can become a reluctant or bored reader at this stage of life. If this happens, your child will fall behind in his or her vocabulary, comprehension, thinking and writing skills. By mid-high school, your teen will be unable to cope with the demands of the curriculum.

IDEAS TO KEEP THE READING FIRES BURNING

- Make sure that reading is still an important *family* event. Keep going to the library together, even if your child doesn't want to be seen with you there. Continue to make the trip a social outing. Let your child invite a friend along and go out afterwards for a hamburger or ice cream.

- Continue to buy books for your child. Take him to a bookstore and offer to pay for something. (Yes, this is bribery, but it works.) Have some ground rules about what you will and won't buy. For example, don't let your child purchase a cartoon collection every single time.

- Don't let the buying of books be an occasional thing. Buy books as often as you can afford. Many parents will fork out big bucks for movie rentals, but balk at the same amount of money going to buy a book. In your home, books must be important enough to purchase constantly.

- Look through the books your child buys or borrows. Ask if you can read some of it with her – although you will probably be told reading together is for babies. So read some of it by yourself, and then discuss the story with your child.

Don't panic if you find something in your child's book that you don't like. Many parents will confiscate a book if they feel it is inappropriate, but this will only pique the child's interest. It is much better to discuss your concerns openly with your child. If you find that you cannot permit your child to finish reading a book that you find offensive, then explain your position clearly and honestly.

Turn off the television. On school nights, tell your child that she can stay up to read, but that there is no TV after such-and-such a time. This sort of rule works best if established at the end of the summer holidays, when even our children are fired up with resolutions about the new school year. If you suddenly put your foot down about television in mid-November, your child will quite likely rebel and call you all sorts of rotten names. Be firm.

Make sure your child still sees you reading. Then talk about your book, magazine or newspaper article.

Why not set aside a family quiet time each day? For a half-hour after dinner, everyone stops what they are doing and reads. Even if you can only accomplish this twice a week, it's worth a try. Your child might complain about it to her friends but, secretly, she will like the belonging feeling it gives her, no matter how quirky.

Recognize that your child will read a variety of materials. He might try reading Tolkien's very long and difficult *The Lord of the Rings* on his own because it is "cool," but then he'll go back to reading superhero comic books.

At this age, kids will read a lot of junk. Don't panic. Ask your child what she likes about this particular book or magazine. Be honest. We have all read throwaway spy thrillers or over-the-top romance novels. We know that this isn't good stuff and so will our children. Remember, at school your child is now studying books as literature and is probably becoming a critical thinker. Encourage this at home.

- Check with your child's teacher or school librarian to see what other kids are reading. Preteens need to fit in with their peers, and your child might be tempted to read if she knows that everybody else is reading a particular book.

- If your child is interested in a television show or a movie that is based on a book, buy the book.

- Don't fret if your child is reading low-quality books. Yes, there are many mass-produced books – usually in series – on the bookshelves, but most kids read them because everyone else is. One mother was worried when she realized that for one year her son had read nothing but a certain horror series for kids. She needn't have been concerned. In grade five, her son wouldn't be caught dead with those "boring" books. He passed them along to his younger brother who, in turn, went through the same phase.

- Ask your child to read to a younger sibling.

- Introduce your child to a new author – preferably one who has written several books. Kids get hooked on an author's style or on a particular series, and will demand to read everything that author has produced.

- Check out what books are being promoted in teen magazines. Often these publications will mention a teen idol's favorite reads. As well, sometimes pamphlets are produced that have famous people talking about: "My favorite book when I was a child was...." Ask your librarian to help you with this one.

- Offer to subscribe to a magazine for your child. Make sure it is age appropriate and "cool."

- Stay involved with your child's homework. Ask about her projects and assignments. Encourage your child to occasionally do his homework at the kitchen table when you're getting dinner ready. This tells your child that you are interested in his life.

Become a member of the Canadian Children's Book Centre. This non-profit organization supports the writing and reading of Canadian children's books. For an inexpensive annual membership, you will receive four newsletters that have up-to-the-minute information about authors and illustrators. You will hear about writing contests for children, and about who has won book awards in Canada. As well, the center produces the annual *Our Choice* catalogue which lists the best books, videos, CD-ROMs and records of the year. An invaluable source of information for you.

SOME FAVORITES TO TEMPT YOUR ALMOST-GROWN-UP CHILD

Preteens are interested in a variety of styles and genres. Here are some of the best Canadian titles. As well as the books mentioned, it's a good bet that your child will love anything else written by these authors.

After the War, by Carol Matas, Scholastic, 1996. The story of a Jewish teenager who survives World War II and embarks on a dangerous journey to a new land.

Amazing Grace: The Story of the Hymn, by Linda Granfield and Janet Wilson, Tundra, 1997. A terrible storm changes the life of slave-trader John Newton. He makes a promise to God, and leaves the hymn *Amazing Grace* as his legacy.

Anne of Green Gables, by Lucy Maud Montgomery, McClelland & Stewart, 1992. First published in 1908, this is *the* Canadian classic known and loved around the world. There are many titles in the *Anne* series, as well as television shows and plays. Be prepared: your child will probably want to visit Prince Edward Island and the Green Gables homestead.

Back of Beyond, by Sarah Ellis, Groundwood, 1996. Stories about teens living ordinary lives, until one startling moment when they catch a glimpse of a world they never knew existed.

Bringing up Beauty, by Sylvia McNicol, Maxwell Macmillan Canada, 1994. A young girl is given the job of raising a puppy until it is old enough to be trained as a seeing eye dog.

The Chicken Doesn't Skate, by Gordon Korman, Scholastic, 1996. A hockey superstar, a dweeb, a young scientist and an animal rights activist all have something in common in this hilarious novel.

Crime Science, by Vivien Bowers, Owl Books, 1997. This way-cool book tells how real-life crime investigators track down criminals.

Daedalus and the Minotaur, by Priscilla Galloway and Normand Cousineau, Annick Press, 1997. Daedalus and his son set out to escape death at King Minos's hands. The third story in the *Tales of Ancient Lands* series.

Discovering the Iceman: What Was It Like to Find a 5,300-year-old Mummy?, by Shelley Tanaka and Laurie McGaw, Scholastic, 1996. In 1991, two hikers discovered the remains of a Stone Age man. Readers are transported back to the Iceman's ancient world. Part of the *I Was There* series.

Falling through the Cracks, by Lesley Choyce, Formac, 1996. Melanie and Trent struggle to stay in high school even though they have both left home.

Glory Days and Other Stories, by Gillian Chan, Kids Can Press, 1996. This collection of short stories looks at five teenagers and their experiences with identity, popularity, power and so on.

Goldstone, by Julie Lawson, Stoddart Kids, 1997. Karin's mother dies suddenly after harsh words were spoken. How can she interpret the dreams Karin has whenever she sleeps with her mother's precious goldstone pendant?

The Hollow Tree, by Janet Lunn, Knopf Canada, 1997. The tale of a young girl who escapes to Canada during the American Revolutionary War. The third novel in the trio that began with *The Root Cellar* and *Shadow in Hawthorn Bay*.

Home Child, by Barbara Haworth-Attard, Roussan, 1996. When 13-year-old Arthur arrives from England in 1914 to work on their farm, Sadie's mother forbids her children to speak "with his kind."

The Jumbo Book of Nature Science, by Pamela Hickman, Kids Can Press, 1996. Using materials found around the home, kids can explore nature with over 100 great activities and experiments.

Laughs: Funny Stories, by Claire Mackay, Tundra, 1997. A humorous collection of 23 poems, stories and riddles.

Little by Little: A Writer's Education, by Jean Little, Penguin, 1987. This is the inspiring autobiography of one of Canada's best-loved authors. Your child will want to read the sequel, *Stars Come Out Within*.

The Maestro, by Tim Wynne-Jones, Groundwood, 1995. A runaway boy in northern Ontario comes across a famous musician who lives alone on a beautiful lake. When the musician dies, the boy searches desperately for a way to keep the cabin.

The Minstrel Boy, by Sharon Stewart, Napoleon, 1997. David Baird, a rock musician, has a motorcycle accident when in Wales with his father. He wakes up in ancient Prydien, and discovers a new path for his music and the source of his troubled dreams.

Moonkid and Prometheus, by Paul Kropp, Stoddart, 1997. Ian (Moonkid) is given the job of tutoring Prometheus. His unorthodox methods help both of them cope with the problems clouding their lives.

One Thing That's True, by Cheryl Foggo, Kids Can Press, 1997. A moving and funny story about family relationships and the consequences of telling helpful lies. Adolescent Roxanne must figure out what acceptance means.

A Pioneer Story, by Barbara Greenwood and Heather Collins, Kids Can Press, 1994. Readers follow the Robertson family through a seasonal cycle of pioneer life on a backwoods farm.

Promise Song, by Linda Holeman, Tundra, 1997. At the turn of the century, thousands of English orphans were "adopted" by Canadians to work on farms and in factories. In this story, two sisters are separated upon arrival in Canada.

Ran Van, a Worthy Opponent, by Diana Wieler, Groundwood, 1995. Rhan knows that he is a knight, Ran Van the Defender. But he discovers that the victories he achieved in Vancouver have not carried over into his new life in Thunder Bay. The sequel to *Ran Van the Defender.*

The Science Book for Girls and Other Intelligent Beings, by Valerie Wyatt, Kids Can Press, 1993. Hands-on activities and experiments show girls how science is a part of everyday life.

The Seven Magpies, by Monica Hughes, HarperCollins, 1996. A young girl, sent to a Scottish boarding school during World War II, uncovers a secret society.

Shadows on a Sword: The Second Book of the Crusades, by Karleen Bradford, HarperCollins, 1996. Theo, a young knight, his friend Amalric and the servant Emma join the Holy Crusade to reclaim Jerusalem. This is the sequel to the award-winning *There Will Be Wolves.*

Silverwing, by Kenneth Oppel, HarperCollins, 1997. Shade is a young silverwing bat who is separated from his colony during the long winter migration. An incredible journey results.

The Sky Is Falling, by Kit Pearson, Penguin, 1989. This first book in the trilogy about Norah and Gavin, an English brother and sister who are sent to Canada during World War II as "war guests." Of course, your child will want to read *Looking at the Moon* and *The Lights Go On Again.*

Strange and Eerie Stories, by Pat Hancock, Scholastic, 1995. Scarey stories to read under the covers at night. Comes with its own mini-light.

The TV Book: A Kid's Guide to Tuning In and Talking Back, by Shelagh Wallace, Annick Press, 1996. A hands-on guide for children to encourage critical television viewing.

Uncle Ronald, by Brian Doyle, Groundwood, 1996. A humorous, tragic story about the memories of 112-year-old Mickey.

Wally Stutzgummer, Super Bad Dude, by Martyn Godfrey, Scholastic, 1992. Wally accepts Krazy Kurt's challenge for a mountain bike race. Everything starts to fall apart for Wally and his friend Carol, but then he finds out what it takes to be a real hero.

One of the *Carol and Wally Books*, and one of the dozens of books by this prolific young adult writer.

Whalesinger, by Welwyn Katz, Groundwood, 1990. This author of several award-winning fantasy books for young people admits that *Whalesinger* is her favorite. It is an adventure-romance taking place at Point Reyes, a spot where Sir Francis Drake landed, close to both the San Andreas Fault and the migration route of the gray whales. The past and present, and the songs of land and ocean mammals intermingle.

Wings to Fly, by Celia Lottridge, Groundwood, 1997. Eleven-year-old Josie, who lives on a homestead in Alberta, is glad when a new girl moves to the area. A sequel to the award-winning *Ticket to Curlew*.

Who Is Frances Rain? by Margaret Buffie, Kids Can Press, 1987. Fifteen-year-old Lizzie is not having a good time on her summer holiday. But then she puts on a child's pair of spectacles she finds in a ruined cabin, and begins to have visions. The first novel in this award-winning writer's career.

Whose Bright Idea Was It?, by Larry Verstraete, Scholastic, 1997. Behind-the-scenes facts, trivia and history about toys, foods, television, skateboards and more.

You Asked? Over 300 Great Questions and Astounding Answers, by Katherine Farris, OWL Books, 1996. Mind-boggling questions submitted over the years by OWL readers.

Bibliography

Babies Need Books, by Dorothy Butler, Atheneum, 1980. Classic book on why and how to read to the youngest infant.

Behind the Story: The Creators of Our Best Children's Books and How They Do It, Barbara Greenwood, Pembroke, 1995. Profiles 23 members of CANSCAIP (Canadian Society of Children's Authors, Illustrators and Performers), giving intriguing insights into how wonderful stories and books are created.

The Good School, by Alan King, Ontario Secondary School Teachers' Federation, 1988. An excellent discussion about what makes a good school.

I'm a Little Teapot, by Jane Cobb, Black Sheep Press, 1996. A selection of the best books, nursery rhymes, fingerplays, songs, games and craft ideas for children.

Literacy Techniques for Building Successful Readers and Writers, by David Booth, Pembroke Publishers, 1996. This flexible resource gives every proven technique for teaching reading and writing.

The New Read-Aloud Handbook, by Jim Trelease, Penguin Books, 1989. How to raise a reader (and bring your family closer together) by reading aloud.

The New Republic of Childhood, by Sheila Egoff and Judith Saltman, Oxford University Press, 1990. Provides an overview of the growth of Canadian children's literature and a comprehensive analysis of each genre.

The Reading Solution, by Paul Kropp, Random House, 1993. Gives down-to-earth, practical advice for parents on making a child a reader for life. Lots of fascinating sidenotes, tips, lists and "did you knows."

Read to Me: Raising Kids Who Love to Read, by Bernice Cullinan, Scholastic, 1992. Loaded with tips for busy parents to encourage reading and writing.

Taking Books to Heart, by Paul Copperman, Addison-Wesley, 1986. Explains the process by which children learn to read at school, and gives parents a home program.

Telling Tales: Storytelling in the Family, by Gail De Vos and Merle Harris, Dragon Hill Publishing, 1995. A fascinating guide to the art of gathering and telling stories.

Why Johnny Can't Read and What You Can Do about It, by Rudolf Franz Flesch, Perennial Library, 1986. Contains material and instructions for teaching children to read at home through phonics. The classic phonics handbook.

Writing Stories, Making Pictures, Canadian Children's Book Centre, 1994. Biographies of 150 Canadian children's authors and illustrators. It is written as a child's resource guide, with helpful, interesting information about when the writer or artist was young.

For fifty years, Coles Notes have been helping students get through high school and university. New Coles Notes will help get you through the rest of life.

Look for these NEW COLES NOTES!

GETTING ALONG IN ...

- French
- Spanish
- Italian
- German
- Russian

HOW-TO ...

- Write Effective Business Letters
- Write a Great Résumé
- Do A Great Job Interview
- Start Your Own Small Business
- Buy and Sell Your Home
- Plan Your Estate

YOUR GUIDE TO ...

- Basic Investing
- Mutual Funds
- Investing in Stocks
- Speed Reading
- Public Speaking
- Wine
- Effective Business Presentations

MOMS AND DADS' GUIDE TO ...

- Basketball for Kids
- Baseball for Kids
- Soccer for Kids
- Hockey for Kids
- Gymnastics for Kids
- Martial Arts for Kids
- Helping Your Child in Math
- Raising A Reader
- Your Child: The First Year
- Your Child: The Terrific Twos
- Your Child: Age Three and Four

HOW TO GET AN A IN ...

- Sequences & Series
- Trigonometry & Circle Geometry
- Senior Algebra with Logs & Exponents
- Permutations, Combinations & Probability
- Statistics & Data Analysis
- Calculus
- Senior Physics
- Senior English Essays
- School Projects & Presentations

NOTES & UPDATES